Hybrid Happiness

Barbara Plester

Hybrid Happiness

Fun and Freedom in Flexible Work

Barbara Plester
Management and International Business
University of Auckland Business School
Auckland, New Zealand

ISBN 978-981-95-2091-6   ISBN 978-981-95-2092-3 (eBook)
https://doi.org/10.1007/978-981-95-2092-3

© The Editor(s) (if applicable) and The Author(s), under exclusive license to Springer Nature Singapore Pte Ltd. 2025

This work is subject to copyright. All rights are solely and exclusively licensed by the Publisher, whether the whole or part of the material is concerned, specifically the rights of translation, reprinting, reuse of illustrations, recitation, broadcasting, reproduction on microfilms or in any other physical way, and transmission or information storage and retrieval, electronic adaptation, computer software, or by similar or dissimilar methodology now known or hereafter developed.
The use of general descriptive names, registered names, trademarks, service marks, etc. in this publication does not imply, even in the absence of a specific statement, that such names are exempt from the relevant protective laws and regulations and therefore free for general use.
The publisher, the authors and the editors are safe to assume that the advice and information in this book are believed to be true and accurate at the date of publication. Neither the publisher nor the authors or the editors give a warranty, expressed or implied, with respect to the material contained herein or for any errors or omissions that may have been made. The publisher remains neutral with regard to jurisdictional claims in published maps and institutional affiliations.

Cover credit: J Studios

This Palgrave Macmillan imprint is published by the registered company Springer Nature Singapore Pte Ltd.
The registered company address is: 152 Beach Road, #21-01/04 Gateway East, Singapore 189721, Singapore

If disposing of this product, please recycle the paper.

This one is for Riki and Maxine. Thank you for so much happiness. Thank you for sharing your children, dogs, chats, thoughts, feelings, laughter, teasing, golf games, puzzles, food by the fire and in the sun. You both bring constant joy, fun, light and laughter into my life.

Preface

Writing this book was frequently a happy process that I was able to carry out in a hybrid form of work—writing mostly at home while having days on-campus in my academic office where I interacted with students and colleagues. Of course, writing is a long, intricate process so not all of it was carried out in peak happiness mode and there were times of frustration, low energy, and moments of thinking that I would never finish. The key to my writing and finishing this book was the very topic that the book is about—hybrid work and finding ways to make it enjoyable, refreshing, and happy while still being productive and thorough. So, while this book is based on my research into fun, humour, play—and now happiness, at the same time it is quite personal in places. As I was writing, I recognised my own hybrid work experience, and I offer my own tips and tricks for hybrid work, detailing how I tailor my personal preferences to support my on-going well-being while working in hybrid mode. Therefore, the book is a blend of personal self-awareness and insights through working in hybrid mode, combined with research findings arising from the analysis of the words, feelings, and experiences of the people I have studied in their workplaces. There are also research points and findings from other sources peppered throughout the chapters, and references are supplied at the end of each chapter to indicate which other studies are cited.

I have not explicitly written about happiness in my prior research because my focus has primarily been upon humour and fun at work and that does not always create happiness—and it can even generate unhappiness. The initial focus for this current research was also humour and fun but the workers I studied clearly linked humour and fun to their own happiness and well-being and so happiness became an important focus of this book. Plus, I have to admit that I find alliteration irresistible and so the title '*Hybrid Happiness*' made me smile while it also seemed to encapsulate how workers felt about their hybrid work.

Like my focus on happiness, I did not set out to write about hybrid work specifically but the research for this book happened within companies where hybrid work was encouraged and where policies had been generated to manage the hybrid process. New policies offered workers official guidance as to company expectations of days at home and days in the office and hybrid work had become a significant factor in the companies that I studied. Therefore, hybridity became the context for this book because during the writing process, hybrid work was evolving and changing how people conducted and perceived their work. While writing this book, hybrid work was also being disestablished in some prominent global corporations that, post-pandemic, ordered workers back-to-the office. This offered an intriguing and fast-changing context for my work-based study.

It is my hope that the notion of happiness and well-being permeates this book, but it is also unrealistic for it to be the only emotive state that workers experience and acknowledge. Therefore, while this book might ostensibly be a quest for happiness and well-being, there is also recognition and articulation of the difficulties, challenges, and issues that simultaneously occur in hybrid work. Enter at your own risk!

Kind regards, Barb

Auckland, New Zealand   Barbara Plester

Acknowledgements

There are many wonderful people who need acknowledging and I sincerely thank them for their contribution to this book.

Firstly, to all of the fantastic participants from the two companies-Firefly and Gecko. Your voices resonate throughout these chapters and your insights, thoughts, and reflections have provided the basis for this work. Even though I cannot name you individually, thank you for sharing your workplaces with me. It was a pleasure to work with you.

To my research partner, Dr. Rhiannon Lloyd, some of our shared work on fun and hybrid work is cited and built upon in this book. Thank you for all your hard work, collegiality, and for making research work fun.

To my former research assistant: Alexandra Venn-Brown, huge thanks for supporting this work in allowing me to use some of the data from your master's thesis: *'Walking on eggshells': Exploratory research on emotions in hybrid work*. Your research was excellent, and it was a pleasure to have you work in the *Fun and well-being in workplace social spaces* project for your master's study. I wish you every success in your stunning new career.

The team at Palgrave Macmillan. Thank you all for your contributions and support and once again it has been a pleasure to work with you all.

My research colleagues at the University of Auckland Business School. The support and debates in our Organisation Studies research group are always highly valuable, and I cherish the times when we work together.

My two faithful canine companions, Bowie and Fergus. You are always snoozing beside me when I'm writing—except when you are barking at something outside the window. You both get a mention in this book, and you add to my own hybrid happiness.

My husband Paul, who works in a home office down the corridor from mine. I love our coffee meetings, lunch breaks, and having a friend in hybrid work. You are my rock, and I cannot thank you enough for all the times you listened to my groans about chapters not working and let me share my half-formed ideas. It seems that when I shared these sticking points with you, they sometimes magically resolved. Thank you for your love and support always.

Thank you to my noisy, fabulous family who bring the love, care, fun, and absolute joy into our home. You make work, and everything else, worthwhile.

Previously Published Material

This book contains previously published excerpts from the Open Access publication: Frontiers of Psychology *Happiness Is 'Being Yourself': Psychological Safety and Fun in Hybrid Work.*

Research information

- The wider research project upon which this book is based is entitled: *Fun and well-being in workplace social spaces.*
- No funding was received for this project.
- The *Fun and well-being in workplace social spaces,* project has ethical clearance from the University of Auckland Ethics Committee: Approved by the University of Auckland Human Participants Ethics Committee on 25 March 2021 **REF: 024713.**
- Please note that pseudonyms are used throughout this book for individual workers and for company names. Identifying details are withheld to protect privacy and confidentiality for workers and workplaces.

Contents

1	**The Quest for Happiness at Work**	1
	Hybrid Work	3
	The Nature of Happiness	4
	Concepts and Contents	5
	Methodological Matters	8
	Being There	8
	Interpretive Approach	10
	Reflexivity	11
	Gathering Data	11
	Analysis Process	12
	Artificial Intelligence (AI)	13
	References	15
2	**Hybrid Hijinks: Where Flexibility Meets Workplace Fun**	17
	What is Workplace Fun?	17
	When Fun Goes Wrong	19
	Fun Experiences in Hybrid Work	21
	Hybrid Fun Enhances Happiness	25
	Gamification	26
	Turning Tasks into Play: Gamification Ideas	27
	Fun Rules	29
	References	29

xiv CONTENTS

3 Fun Reimagined: People and Culture in the Hybrid Workplace — 31
- Organisational Culture and Climate — 31
- Two Fun Companies — 33
  - Gecko — 34
  - Firefly — 35
- Humour, Fun, and Play. What's the Difference? — 36
  - Fun — 37
  - Humour — 37
  - Play — 38
- A Fun Framework — 39
  - Managed Fun — 39
  - Organic Fun — 40
  - Task Fun — 40
- Fun and Flexibility — 41
- Hybrid Fun and Games — 44
- Artefacts of Fun: What Happened to Ping Pong? — 45
- Happiness in Hybrid Culture — 48
- References — 49

4 Psychological Safety in Hybrid Fun — 51
- Safe versus Unsafe Fun — 51
- Psychological Safety — 53
- Fun Climate — 54
- Risky Fun — 55
- Just Be Yourself! — 61
- Leading Fun — 62
- A Complex Relationship — 65
- References — 68

5 The Emotional Landscape of Hybrid Work — 71
- Emotions — 71
- Emotion versus Mood — 72
- Emotional Dynamics at Work — 72
- Emotional Connection, Disconnection, and Everything Between — 74
- Decoding Emotional Expression — 77
- Letting Emotions Show — 79
- Back-to-the-Office Mandates — 81
- Autonomy: The Key to Hybrid Happiness — 82
- References — 83

6	**Being Happy and Hybrid**	85
	Happiness	85
	Happiness at Work	86
	Workplace Well-Being	89
	Well-Being without Walls	92
	Happiness Hacks	93
	References	95
7	**Tech-Powered Freedom**	97
	Tech that Works Where You Do	97
	The Trials and Tribulations of Tech	98
	The Power of Trust	99
	Balancing Connection and Disconnection	102
	Boundaries Matter	103
	'Gerald You're on Mute!'	105
	Surviving Hybrid Like a Boss	106
	References	108
8	**Hybrid Happily Ever After?**	111
	The Quest Never Ends	111
	Rewind and Recap	112
	Hybrid Intelligence: Tomorrow's Workplace Weapon	114
	References	116

About the Author

Dr. Barbara Plester is Associate Professor in the Department of Management and International Business (MIB) at the University of Auckland Business School. She also serves as Associate Dean Equity, Diversity and Inclusion for the Business Faculty. She received her Ph.D. in Management from Massey University in 2008 and has worked at the University of Auckland since 2007. In 2018 she was awarded Senior Fellowship of the Higher Education Academy (SFHEA). She is a board member of the Australasian Humour Studies Network (AHSN). Her research explores workplace humour, fun, play, wellbeing, gender effects, technological behaviour, food rituals and the challenges and contradictions of workplace interactions. She is currently researching the impact of hybrid work on humour/fun/play, socializing, ethics, and well-being. Within her department Barbara belongs to the Organization Studies research group, and she teaches critical management, organizational theory, and qualitative methodology at undergraduate and postgraduate levels. Prior to her academic career, Barbara worked in Publishing and Information Technology companies and has experience in Sales, Marketing and HRM.

Abbreviations

AI	Artificial Intelligence
CEO	Chief Executive Officer
CHO	Chief Happiness Officer
HR	Human Resources
NDA	Non-disclosure Agreement
PSC	Psychologically Safe Climate
Psych	Psychological
R&D	Research and Development
Tech	Technology
VPN	Virtual Private Network
WFH	Working From Home
WLB	Work-Life Balance

CHAPTER 1

The Quest for Happiness at Work

Hi, and thanks for choosing to read this book about happiness in hybrid work. Happiness has been considered to be the 'holy grail' of workplace research as people seek justification for the assumption that a happy worker is a productive worker (Sender et al., 2021). After nearly one hundred years of studies, there is still no conclusive evidence for this assumption and worker happiness continues to be a complex and intriguing topic for positive psychology researchers. While organisations might be expected to keep their workers happy through providing optimal conditions, this can be hard to achieve as workers have individual likes and preferences. However, attempting to foster and encourage positive workplace behaviours that improve workers well-being and happiness can have some valuable outcomes for a company and for the individual worker.

Hybrid work is increasingly one of the ways that enhance working conditions for many people through offering the autonomy and flexibility to conduct work in shared spaces such as offices, and also to work remotely—most often through working from home (WFH). A recent study shows that flexible work positively and significantly influences workers' work-life balance (WLB) and this can enhance happiness, especially for those with family responsibilities (Martínez & Chunga-Liu, 2023). It is this idea of finding, creating, and enhancing worker happiness in hybrid work that is the underpinning thesis of this book. Happiness is nuanced and complex, and so are the social dynamics of hybrid work. This book

© The Author(s), under exclusive license to Springer Nature
Singapore Pte Ltd. 2025
B. Plester, *Hybrid Happiness*,
https://doi.org/10.1007/978-981-95-2092-3_1

does indeed feel like a quest for the holy grail of workplace happiness, but as a worker who feels on-going happiness in how I am able to work, and through my research with many interesting and insightful workers, I feel optimistic about attempting this quest in the pages that follow.

While I cannot guarantee your personal happiness after reading this book, I can share my research findings, my personal tips, and some insights into the social science principles and underlying assumptions, values, and practices that are emerging in hybrid work models. I had fun writing this book (most days) and I did write from my desk at home most of the time with a few stints in my campus office. When writing at home I used all sorts of techniques and micro breaks to enhance my well-being and to encourage myself to keep going. Micro breaks to do fun things were my incentive and these included trips to my local café for coffee, walks on the beach, playing with my dogs, word puzzles—to name just a few activities that I interspersed with my work at home. For me, the variety of fun activities increased my mental and physical health, well-being, and enjoyment in the discipline of writing continuously. Hopefully it also improved this book!

I planned for the book to take 15 months of writing that would occur alongside my other academic activities. Unfortunately, during the writing process I broke my ankle by tripping over one of my two large dogs while I was bustling around home one Saturday morning. Turns out that wooden floors make for hard landings! Recovery took about eight weeks, and I was glad (and lucky) that I have the type of job where I could mostly stay at home and recover from my injury although I did traverse campus twice a week on crutches to teach my large undergraduate management class. To be honest, although teaching on crutches was challenging, I enjoyed this social contact with my lively, engaged students as a contrast from the quiet days at home, writing, planning and working remotely. The disadvantage of a broken ankle was that it slowed down the writing process as pain and tiredness forced me to rest more than I would normally. Thanks to the team at Pan MacMillan who graciously allowed me to extend the deadline for this book that has taken two years to complete.

I share this personal story not to illustrate my on-going clumsiness but because it is an example of working flexibly and being able to work in a hybrid manner, which was a real bonus when I was injured, and my work was somewhat compromised. My writing process was a living example of the benefits and convenience of hybrid work. For those people managing on-going disabilities or injuries, both hidden and overt, I hope that you have the flexibility and support to work in way that promotes your well-being and happiness. Hybrid work supported by technological tools is increasingly popular and viable for many, but not all, workers. In the coming chapters I will explore some significant and even unexpected dynamics of working this way.

Hybrid Work

Injuries aside, I am lucky enough to have the privilege of working in a hybrid format for my job as an Associate Professor at a university. I wrote this book under the hybrid work conditions that I have researched, and I will discuss these in greater depth in the chapters ahead. For all of my time working at the university I have been able to work some days at home and others on campus—the mix is discretionary to me, but I must be present on campus to teach and for some key activities and meetings. Currently my usual pattern is to work two or three days at home and spend the others on campus depending on my commitments for each week. For example, the week when I was writing this introduction felt quite relaxed as I worked three days at home (writing and preparing teaching content) and attended campus for two days. Hybrid work is a flexible way of working that combines remote work (offsite) with work that occurs in person with co-located colleagues. Usually, this creates choices for employees who can nominate days that they will work at home and days when they will attend the office. In effect, a hybrid work model seems to offer the best of both worlds allowing flexibility and autonomy for remote work as well as collaboration and structure in the office setting. Recent research suggests that when employees spend two days at home and three in the office, they tend to opt for Mondays and Fridays at home, with the three middle weekdays spent in the office and this is sometimes called the '3–2' model. A common variant is the 2–3 model where the emphasis is transposed into three days at the physical workspace and two WFH and of course workers may be able to negotiate multiple different versions depending on their work demands and workplace policies.

Hybrid work is not new, and people were working this way before the COVID 19 pandemic. However, many workers had to adjust to working from home during lockdown restrictions. Both managers and workers mostly found that this was manageable and experienced some distinct advantages such as gaining extra time through not commuting, and the extra comfort of adopting a relaxed dress code when WFH was enjoyed by many. Numerous workplaces, including businesses and not-for-profit organisations have maintained the option for hybrid work after the pandemic and have even formalised their hybrid work policies. However, more recently, several globally renowned companies have insisted that employees return to offices fulltime. Thus, the foundation for this book is complex and contradictory at times, and I will carefully examine features and advantages of hybrid work alongside issues, concerns, and emerging changes.

While hybrid work includes a form of remote work, usually working from home, fully remote work is a type of work where employees exclusively work offsite and may include WFH or being situated in different places, or it may be a mobile form of work involving travel. Both forms rely heavily on digital communication tools including access to the internet and using a range of different devices depending on work requirements and there is an entire Chapter 7 that discusses technological impacts and challenges.

The Nature of Happiness

The title of this book includes the term 'happiness' and from my research into this area through my humour and fun research, I have found that it is a complex and multifaceted emotion that can be defined in numerous ways. It can be perceived as a mixture of positive emotions that may result in satisfaction, joy, and contentment. Philosophers such as Aristotle debated happiness, and arguments have raged for centuries especially in the field of ethics. Some philosophers view happiness as the goal of human life and Aristotle claimed that living a meaningful and virtuous life leads to true happiness. Other philosophers contend that happiness is linked to seeking and achieving pleasure while avoiding pain. There is much philosophical and ethical debate about happiness including arguments that suggest happiness comes second to moral duty, with utilitarianism doctrines claiming that happiness has intrinsic value and actions should promote the greatest good for the greatest number of people.

Biological arguments link happiness to the release of chemicals in the brain such as dopamine, serotonin, and endorphins, while social scientists focus on social aspects of happiness such as community, relationships, and a sense of belonging. Of course, there are also cultural differences in what is meant by happiness with some cultures highlighting personal achievement and success, while others prioritise collective harmony and community. There are multiple complex ethical, cultural, and biological arguments debating happiness but here I simply want to acknowledge that they all contribute to everyday modern conceptions of happiness. Positive psychology perspectives on happiness and its' interrelationship with well-being and hybrid work will be outlined in Chapter 6.

It is beyond the scope of this book to fully explore the variety of perspectives in happiness research and scholarship and so the two paragraphs above offer brief, simplifications of some key arguments. It is reasonable to say that no one has categorically defined happiness or what creates happiness, but that most people hope to experience happiness throughout their overall lives and in their work. This book will consider happiness, or the lack thereof, in the context of hybrid work in a series of differently themed chapters. Before moving into a synopsis of each chapter, I conclude this section with a quote from one of my research participants about her view of hybrid work as a factor of happiness and well-being. She manages a large team of people who are empowered to work from home some days while attending in-office days for either two or three days a week. It is notable that I did not explicitly ask her about happiness, but enquired about the hybrid work model for her team:

> And I have people having working, regular working from home arrangements, part time, different style hours. And then what I find is, it brings loyalty, discretionary effort - hybrid people are happy. And I mean, of course, it's a well-being thing because things are so unmanageable these days. It makes it more manageable. We have got that flexibility. I think we were going that way. COVID just hurried us along, right? (Rose, Firefly).

CONCEPTS AND CONTENTS

This book is organised into eight chapters including this introduction, a concluding Chapter 8, and six themed chapters in between. Chapters comprise key ideas that I have identified in my recent research into fun, humour, and hybrid work. This introductory chapter entitled: *The quest for happiness at work* introduces the context for the book and discusses the increasingly popular adoption of hybrid work following the global pandemic and technological advancements. The concept of happiness is briefly introduced, chapter topics are outlined, and my methodological and research processes are detailed (below).

Although the book explores the notion of happiness throughout, this has never been the explicit focus of my research enquiries. For many years I have studied the concepts of humour and fun in workplaces and the surrounding constructs that create the conditions for humour and fun to flourish or (sadly) wither in some circumstances. My engagement with the related concept of happiness was coincidental but perhaps inevitable because in my research explorations, workers talk about fun, humour, happiness, games and play in an integrated and holistic way that cannot always be separated out. Therefore, throughout the coming chapters I will discuss happiness via my lens of humour and fun and I offer data extracts from participants where happiness may be explicit or simply inferred through their responses and my analytical interpretations.

Chapter 2 presents '*Hybrid hijinks: Where flexibility meets workplace fun*' and opens with definitions of fun. This chapter investigates tensions in fun and details how fun is experienced individually by different people which highlights the essential subjectivity and individuality that workers bring to the concept of workplace fun. Forced fun and fun that goes wrong is discussed using workplace examples. The impact of fun in hybrid work is specifically addressed before the chapter concludes with sections on gamification with workplace examples of gamification.

Chapter 3, '*Fun reimagined: People and culture in the hybrid workplace*' specifically spotlights the social aspects of hybrid work, fun, and happiness and how these are underpinned by the key concepts of organisational culture and climate. The title is an acknowledgement of People and Culture teams and managers who seemed to feel extra responsibility for promoting, creating, and monitoring fun and happiness at work, centering their focus on worker well-being. This chapter explores changes in workplace events and activities, detailing the impact of changes upon the social interactions of workers and managers. It explores strategies adopted by People and Culture teams, or HR managers and senior leaders in their attempts to maintain and promote collegiality, collaboration, and fun as artefacts of a thriving organisational culture in companies that permit hybrid work.

Chapter 4, '*Psychological safety in hybrid fun*', addresses the need for psychological safety when participating in workplace fun and humour. This chapter develops the idea that psychological safety is important in hybrid work and especially so when it comes to participating in fun and play activities. Psychological safety is a shared belief, held by a team or wider group, that it is safe to share ideas, concerns, ask questions, admit mistakes and speak up without fearing negative consequences. This is important when deciding whether to opt in, or out, of fun activities. Fun shared in hybrid work may involve sharing personal information, photos, views of one's home and family, or articulating alternative viewpoints, laughable mistakes, and the lighter side of work. All of this requires psychological safety, and this concept is rarely linked to notions of fun, play, and humour at work.

Chapter 5, '*The emotional landscape of hybrid work*', is concerned with the emotional aspects of hybrid work and how this can be complicated when workplace communication is online. While hybrid work offers workers freedom and flexibility it also evokes frustration and anxiety. This chapter explores the emotional gamut of hybrid work including empathy, care, frustration and joy. Reading others' emotions online is complex and raises questions about emotional regulation and emotional labour. As emotions are increasingly expressed through technological channels, new forms of language such as emojis or pictograms are often used to illustrate feelings and as a substitute for in-person emotional cues. Pictorial language builds liveliness into textual conversations and can indicate fun, play and humour ☺ but these can easily be misconstrued and misread.

Chapter 6, '*Being happy and hybrid*', builds upon Chapter 5 in its exploration of the emotion of happiness at work and specifically in hybrid work. It covers the interrelated areas of well-being and work-life balance (WLB). This chapter explores happiness and the impacts for well-being in hybrid work, debating challenges and benefits, family dynamics, the joys of not commuting, self-management, and the importance of breaks. Additionally, this chapter depicts the physical embodiment of flexible work contrasting the physical aspects of home offices to workplace office environments.

Chapter 7, '*Tech-powered freedom*', outlines technology protocols asking whether hybrid workers are 'always on'? It explores connection versus disconnection, trust, and questions the spectre of monitoring and surveillance. It outlines the lighter side of online meetings asking: What's going on in the chat? The chapter depicts how fun, and humour can be portrayed in informal online channels such as Slack or Kahoot while different platforms may be used to conduct more formal and larger meetings. The chapter concludes with some helpful hints and practical points to consider in online meetings which are an essential part of most hybrid work.

Chapter 8, '*Hybrid happily ever after?*' is the final chapter bringing the book to a close with summaries of key points and speculations about the future of work and how hybrid work might change and evolve. The one thing that is certain is that there will be changes and probably they will be fast paced. Although technological changes are more or less guaranteed, new ways of working are likely to generate a host of new relational behaviours, and this will involve changes to the ways that people experience fun and social interaction at work. Future hybrid work may look quite different, but workers will still need happiness, fun, humour and playful games and these may take very different forms from current versions. Hopefully the future will be socially rewarding, fun, and mostly happy.

METHODOLOGICAL MATTERS
Being There

I am an ethnographic researcher. Ethnography is a form of qualitative research that has a focus on the social relations within a site and can involve a researcher immersing themselves into a community or organisation to observe and understand behaviour from a close standpoint. I like to simplify this by calling it 'research by hanging around'. I find this ethnographic immersion to be a useful approach to my research because humour and fun are highly contextual and complex, and I have always felt that the epithet 'you have to be there' applies to understanding why people might laugh or have fun in workplace situations. There is a lot going on in humour and fun events and interactions including tone, facial expressions, gestures and a myriad of nuanced behaviours. Therefore, I try to capture this richness and detail by being there. Of course, I do not always see or hear all fun and humour and so some of it is told to me in stories or reminiscences by participants, so my research is a blend of first-person impressions garnered by me as researcher, combined with description, narratives, and insights from workplace participants.

In my research I immerse myself within an organisation for about one full month, and during that time assimilate so that I become like a staff member, and I undertake some small workplace activities, join meetings and events, and in general behave like everyone else in the organisation.

Depending on the access granted, I usually set myself up in an open-plan area and work on my laptop whilst also taking notes of activities around me, asking questions of people as they arise, and arranging interviews with those that agree to talk to me. The first few days can be quiet as people get used to me in their space but usually after three days people start to talk to me and even volunteer as interview subjects. Of course, I supply my university ethics consent forms and do not overly persuade or coerce people into being involved in the research. I am fully transparent about what I am doing in the workplace and offer documents explaining the project to everyone. I also make it very clear if anyone is uncomfortable with me observing them or their work activities, I can move or remove observations and comments that I have noted. This also applies to interviews where participants sign a consent form that advises them that they can withdraw their information by a specific date. I have been lucky in that no one has ever asked me to remove data or myself, and I have found that many people enjoy sharing information about themselves and their workplace, often pointing out features or checking that I have observed and noted interesting activities. I treat this access and openness with complete respect, and I take care not to identify participants or their workplaces, sometimes omitting details if they have the possibility to compromise confidentiality. Most companies ask me to sign a Non-disclosure Agreement (NDA) in case I inadvertently see or hear important information that must not be disclosed. All company or participants names used in this book (or any of my publications) are pseudonyms.

I took a grounded theory approach to this ethnographic research which simply means that I did not start with any specific hypothesis of what I would find, rather I let the findings emerge organically as the study progressed. This is how my research on fun and humour has developed into a book about happiness, because participants conflated these ideas and constantly linked them. My approach allowed me the freedom to ask further questions and explore when I saw or heard something that seemed interesting and significant. Similarly, this is how I came to write about hybrid happiness because through my data collection process a new focus on hybrid work emerged with people noting that it made them happy (for the most part). When I immersed myself in companies, I simply expected to research humour and fun in their everyday office operations but instead I found that my studied companies were operating hybrid formats and that this had significant impacts on humour and fun and the workers linked hybrid work with happiness. As the workers strongly aligned happiness with hybrid work, I needed to explore both of these concepts in the data analysis for this book and also in other related publications from the research. This resulted in some interesting new research pathways and findings into online humour and fun, an aspect that I have not fully researched in past studies. Since conducting the research, I have published papers on psychological safety in hybrid fun/humour and a more recently published paper discussing '*New Frontiers of Fun*' in the Employee Relations journal, that explores how fun is different in hybrid models of work (see references at the end of each chapter for details of where these may be accessed).

Interpretive Approach

An interpretive approach works well with my ethnographic preferences as it focuses on the context of the research and how different participants, researchers, and analysts make sense of events, occurrences, and everyday fun/humour interactions. Interpretivism can bring in symbolic meanings, sensemaking, interchanges of thoughts and feelings, and lived experience of both researcher and research subjects. It is a useful approach to explore complex and ambiguous experiences in context and allows me to consider multiple meanings and insights (Frechette et al., 2020). Another strength of interpretive research is the opportunity to highlight multiple voices (known as 'polyphony') which gives many participants a 'voice' in the findings presented (Eatough et al., 2008). I usually achieve this polyphony by providing multiple verbatim extracts from interviews or extracts from my onsite observations.

Interpretivism acknowledges my role as researcher and admits that some of the meanings derived from the research arise from my own depth of understanding of the topic, combined with deep analysis of the data gathered. I do note that although I am writing this current book individually, often I work with other researchers, and we independently analyse my collected data and then compare our interpretations and findings in a collaborative process that helps to support important or significant knowledge development. This helps to discover intricate layers of meaning that enhance our overall understanding of the topic (Frost et al., 2010). Data used to support the assertions in this book, although mostly collected by myself, has all been through this multi-layered process and analysed in conjunction with academic colleagues—acknowledged at the forefront of this book. A small amount of data used in Chapter 5 originated from an associated project undertaken by my master's student Alexandra Venn-Brown and she has kindly allowed me to use her data in this book.

Reflexivity

As an interpretive researcher it is important for me to acknowledge my own role in the research because my own beliefs, experiences, and assumptions do influence the research to some extent (Dowling, 2006; Frechette et al., 2020). Therefore, having academic colleagues also analyse my data helps to mitigate my own influence on results. I try to keep a strong self-awareness to the forefront when doing research and check that my interpretations are realistic and not reflecting the outcome that I expect to see. I use journaling as part of this research process, documenting my personal impressions, state of mind, feelings, and reactions while in the field collecting data. When I review these notes, it brings the in-the-field experiences back in powerful way that helps me remember the significant features and moments of research.

Oftentimes I also use a technique called 'member checking' whereby I write a report summarising findings from one organisation, then make a time to present this report in-person to the group or groups that were studied. This is usually highly enjoyable, and I have found that workplace participants seem to relish hearing about themselves in this way. This offers an opportunity for a robust (and often hilarious) debate and people give their reactions to the results presented. I have found this to be really useful and often leave a session such as this with even greater insights and understanding as organisational members may elaborate or extend on what I interpreted about them and their culture. So far all of my studied organisations have stated that they found this helpful and the insights were valid, 'on point', and useful to their on-going cultural development.

Gathering Data

By now, you will have gleaned that I use multiple methods to gather data within organisations. This offers diverse perspectives that enhance transparency and understanding, allowing me to capture some of the complexity of organisational life (Frost et al., 2010; Easterby-Smith et al.,

2008). When designing research projects, I aim to establish a strong, relevant connection to the everyday life of those I study, and I prioritise depth and richness of data over quantity and quantifiable measures (Easterby-Smith et al., 2008). This is who I am as a researcher, and I have worked this way for all of the twenty years of my research career.

The most recent data used to underpin much of this book were gathered from two different organisations. I did have several other places lined up to study but the Covid pandemic intervened and post-covid some of my companies were reluctant to admit visitors to their worksites. Fair enough. Both data collections occurred over a period of four full-immersion weeks. Study one was within a technology company I have called 'Gecko' and the second study was conducted in a food manufacturing organisation (code-named 'Firefly'). I undertook the data collection solo, fully immersed in both companies and I completed 31 semi-structured, in-depth interviews with workers from all levels including CEOs and senior staff as well as very junior, newly employed staff. More than 20 hours of audio recording were transcribed using Otter.ai software. I made participant observations in both organisations and was also granted access to some online platforms such as Slack and Kahoot, where I collected and analysed further data from online conversations and exchanges, many about events, fun and humorous happenings. This all produced a huge amount of rich information leading to some insights and new understandings about fun, humour and hybrid work.

Analysis Process

I use different types of analysis systems depending on what I am planning to do with the data, and my analysis is driven by how I am going to present and write about it. However, these are mostly within two or three different analysis systems that suit my interpretive approach, either a coded, thematic analysis, narrative analysis, or discourse analysis. Thematic analysis is quite structured and involves repeatedly working through transcribed interview transcripts, observation notes, and online data and coding different chunks of information into multiple different categories (Braun & Clarke, 2006, 2013). Coding is repetitive and gradually moves from a fairly open system where there are a huge number of potential categories, into more refined stages of coding as key ideas and significant ideas begin to emerge. Although there are sophisticated software programmes available for these processes, I prefer to be really hands-on with the data and work manually creating a series of tables that are constantly changing with additions and deletions as stories emerge from the data. Sometimes stories are used for narrative analyses and if doing discourse analysis, I explore what the words are doing, and how they are actively used to construct meaning for the workers.

After much repetition and revisiting I start to look for patterns in the data. Sometimes there are strong agreements and overlap, and sometimes there are big differences and tensions. This makes data analysis an intriguing and even exciting part of my research process, although it does take a lot of time and effort. After identifying patterns, discourses, and different voices, I can start to link the data to theory that relates to the ideas and I can link multiple participant stories, extracts, or even a few words together to explore common threads, while also considering the dissenting voices and what they might mean. These styles of analysis work well with the type of data I collect and showcasing multiple voices by using extracts from different people, makes the theoretical points much more interesting. I do not alter any of the words when presenting such extracts, even when they may have used profanity or colourful phrasing. You will encounter extracts of data throughout all of the following chapters.

Artificial Intelligence (AI)

AI is changing the way we work, research, learn, and teach. Transparency is important to me and so I am declaring here my limited use of AI in researching information for this book. I resisted using AI for quite a while as authenticity is important to me and I hope to create nuance and even emotional connection throughout this book. I also had ethical issues regarding transparency and trust issues about the quality of content generated by AI. This resulted in my discovery of a new concept that I (and others) have labelled 'AI guilt'. This refers to moral or ethical concerns that AI is helping perform tasks that had always been solely completed by humans. According to AI itself, it is a common feeling in academic, professional, and creative contexts that value individuality and originality. Here is a quote from AI, generated when I asked Microsoft co-pilot: What is AI guilt?

AI guilt highlights the complex relationship between human intellect and machine capabilities, prompting users to question the essence of learning, creativity, and personal achievement (Microsoft co-pilot).

As I am increasingly expected to use AI in my teaching and to help business students learn to use AI in preparation for the future world of work they will enter, it seemed clear that I needed to get over my resistance and my AI guilt. AI also offered me eight different ways of coping with AI guilt that included setting clear boundaries and communicating transparently about how AI is used in my work. With these points in mind here is my declaration of how I have used AI in this book.

Firstly, I used an AI programme to transcribe my audio recordings of interviews with workplace participants. This saved me a lot of time but was not a perfect process, so I had to check each textual transcript and ensure that the words from the workers were transcribed as truly and authentically as possible. Voice recognition is improving quickly but still struggles with interpreting every word and phrase accurately.

I had conducted all the data collection in person and was working with my findings in multiple ways as I began work on this book. However, I was also aware that my qualitative research work does not cover wide expanses of people and companies but instead offers in-depth, nuanced, and rich accounts of the people and companies that I research. So, I used AI to cover a wider terrain and to check my findings. Each heading or key idea I wrote about, I then checked on AI and asked questions such as 'what am I missing here?' or 'are there other factors or ideas that should be considered?' AI became my verifying tool, and I used it as a wide-ranging search engine that gave me validation and some extension of my key ideas. At times there were points that I had not covered so if I felt they were useful, I added them to my writing. I used AI as another tool in my research arsenal, simply treating it as a sophisticated search engine. I did occasionally ask AI to reword my boring titles, but I never really liked the ideas it threw out which were often elaborate, fanciful and not really my style. From the AI responses I simply used some of the generated ideas, to rebuild my own original ideas further.

Please be assured, the writing is all mine. AI is good at clearly presenting key bullet points, but I wrote everything in my own words to preserve my own voice and tone throughout the book. The data examples and quotes used are from actual participants and none of these were AI generated. Therefore, I acknowledge my use of AI as a research tool that offers checks and balances to my own research perspectives and interpretations. AI itself claims that it is a 'valuable partner in my creative journey'. While a valuable tool, I'm not prepared to give it the status of 'partner'— a term I reserve for my human research collaborators, acknowledged at the front of this book.

REFERENCES

Braun, V., & Clarke, V. (2006). Using thematic analysis in psychology. *Qualitative Research in Psychology, 3*(2), 77–101.

Dowling, M. (2006). Approaches to reflexivity in qualitative research. *Nurse Researcher, 13*(3), 7–21.

Easterby-Smith, M., Golden-Biddle, K., & Locke, K. (2008). Working With Pluralism: Determining Quality in Qualitative Research. *Organizational Research Methods, 11*(3), 419–429. https://doi.org/10.1177/1094428108315858

Eatough, V., Smith, J. A., Willig, C., & Stainton-Rogers, W. (2008). *The SAGE Handbook of Qualitative Research in Psychology* (pp. 179–194). SAGE Publications.

Frechette, J., Bitzas, V., Aubry, M., Kilpatrick, K., & Lavoie-Tremblay, M. (2020). Capturing lived experience: Methodological considerations for interpretive phenomenological inquiry. *International Journal of Qualitative Methods, 19*. https://doi.org/10.1177/1609406920907254

Frost, N., Nolas, S. M., Brooks-Gordon, B., Esin, C., Holt, A., Mehdizadeh, L., & Shinebourne, P. (2010). Pluralism in qualitative research: The impact of different researchers and qualitative approaches on the analysis of qualitative data. *Qualitative Research, 10*(4), 441–460.

Martínez, L. E. H., & Chunga-Liu, Z. E. (2023). Job happiness: Influence of work flexibility through work-life balance and gender moderation. *Journal of Management Development, 43*(2), 187–199.

Microsoft. (2025). *Copilot (Version: Chat interface)* [Large language model]. https://copilot.microsoft.com/

Sender, G., Nobre, G. C., Armagan, S., & Fleck, D. (2021). In search of the Holy Grail: A 20-year systematic review of the happy-productive worker thesis. *International Journal of Organisational Analysis, 29*(5), 1199–1224.

CHAPTER 2

Hybrid Hijinks: Where Flexibility Meets Workplace Fun

What is Workplace Fun?

Fun provides amusement, pleasure and enjoyment and can invoke happiness. It can make you smile, laugh, feel lighter, and can even energise people. It can be something that is relaxing or adventurous or silly, can include games, competitions, play, and creativity as well as cracking jokes and socialising.

Workplace fun is a complex blend of social interaction, pleasurable activities, and playfulness. It is supposed to create enjoyment, amusement, and light-hearted pleasure (Tews et al., 2014). Fun is closely linked to humour and laughter and can mitigate boredom at work, offer a refreshing break or distraction, foster a sense of belonging, and can be a way of relieving stress, tension, and pressure in modern workplaces. Some early studies into fun and humour at work were conducted within factory conditions and a game involving stealing co-workers' bananas was the focus of an early study entitled '*Banana Time*' (Roy, 1959), showing that fun was significant in relieving boredom and tension. Another early shop-floor study (Burawoy, 1979) showed that fun and games improved worker performance in factory conditions.

There is a huge range of potential fun-filled activities for workplaces ranging from team-building activities and challenges (building rafts used to be popular)—to celebrating at work for birthdays, achievements, and milestones. Some workplaces have creative breaks designed to foster

© The Author(s), under exclusive license to Springer Nature Singapore Pte Ltd. 2025
B. Plester, *Hybrid Happiness*,
https://doi.org/10.1007/978-981-95-2092-3_2

innovation, relaxation, and enjoyment, while others organise elaborate activities such as dress-up days, parties, quizzes, fun competitions, and challenges to stimulate friendly rivalry and excitement.

Experiences of fun are subjective and what constitutes fun is different for each person (Plester, 2009). The complexity comes from this individual interpretation of what constitutes fun. For some it is a bit of light-hearted banter at work while for others fun is an event or activity that is organised or spontaneously occurs to stimulate pleasure and social interaction. Fun can also be experienced in work tasks that are enjoyable, and people may achieve a state of flow, where time passes without them realising it due to their full engagement and pleasure in the activity. However, there are also people who do not consider fun to be part of their work life and see it as inappropriate and irrelevant in the workplace. I have met all of these types of people and always ask workers what fun at work means for them. I often extend my questioning and ask workers and managers about their team or group and whether they have any specific fun times, experiences, or activities.

The internet is rife with sites with titles promoting '20 ways to have fun at work with employees' (How to Have Fun at Work with Employees: 20 Ideas [https://teambuilding.com/blog/fun-at-work]) and these suggest activities such as pet days, photo competitions, hobby days, pranks, fancy dress days, and celebrations. Now that hybrid work is becoming more popular and embedded in workplaces, there are similar sites extolling virtual team-building and fun ideas (26 Best Virtual Team Celebration Ideas for Work [https://teambuilding.com/blog/virtual-team-celebration]). One site even suggests an activity including a tiny campfire with s'mores—where workers are sent a s'mores kit with a candle and then team members meet online, and workers make their own s'mores while sharing stories as if 'around the campfire'. Other virtual fun activities include the ever-popular online quizzes, riddle challenges, and virtual treasure hunts. (50 Fun Activities to Boost Engagement with Remote and Hybrid Teams [https://www.hrmorning.com/wp-content/uploads/2022/05/50-Fun-Activities-to-Boost-Engagement-with-Remote-and-Hybrid-Teams_Preciate.pdf]).

Both virtual and in-office fun activities range from simple games to very elaborate set-ups involving kits and resources either given to workers or sent to their home (another example is cookie decorating kits). In contrast to such elaborate performances of workplace fun, everyday fun may comprise simple organic interactions involving light-hearted chat and humour. Some fun times require complex organisation while other fun times just occur naturally and spontaneously and this conception of organic versus managed fun will be further explored in Chapter 3. Although fun is usually well-intentioned and promoted to increase camaraderie and happiness, due to its subjective nature and the multiple individual differences of workers, it has the potential to backfire or fail to engage some people and can be experienced as time-wasting or even may be considered offensive. In other words, unfortunately fun can go horribly wrong and I have encountered several such episodes, some of these I observed, and other 'bad fun' incidents were recounted in detail by aggrieved workers.

When Fun Goes Wrong

Fun is not universally enjoyed by people at work and can be seen as patronising and can even cause cynicism for workers (Fleming, 2005). There is sometimes pressure for workers to participate and enjoy fun even when they do not enjoy a particular activity. I first encountered antipathy towards fun in my early research when I asked a worker (Fletcher) about fun at work. He told me of a time at a previous company where a fun day was announced where all employees were expected to dress up as their favourite TV or movie character. He was appalled by this activity which he thought was embarrassing and childish, so he simply elected to stay at home that day. This is exactly the opposite of what was intended by the activity that had been created as light-hearted silliness for team-bonding and enjoyment, yet for Fletcher, it resulted in absenteeism—definitely not the desired management outcome!

Fletcher's experience illustrates the individual assessment of what is fun and the difficulty in planning activities that will be considered to be fun by most workers. Additionally, it shows the pressure that can be placed on workers to participate because Fletcher felt that his only option to avoid a distasteful activity, was to stay at home, taking sick leave to do so. For Fletcher, it seemed a better option to take a sick day than risk turning up to work and be seen avoiding participating in something that he thought was demeaning or participating only minimally while feeling supremely uncomfortable.

Another young worker described having to sing Christmas Carols at work in December and when expressing her desire not to participate was accused of being 'not a team player' so she reluctantly participated. This is where organising fun for workers gets really tricky and complex. It may not be possible to cater to all tastes especially if some workers are highly introverted. This tension is aptly described by Josie in discussing a fun activity at her work during the Christmas season:

> ...like for example, when we had our Christmas party...I was very much hesitant to go because I know I don't know what's going to happen but yeah - introverted me - it's Friday I just want to stay at home, but I went there because I want to know what's how it is done. And then apparently it is talking, drinking, eating, having chatter so I stay there I engage with them. But again, introverted me - I am not into small chats and it's very loud for me and therefore not - it's not - I'm feeling not comfortable anymore. So, an hour of really engaging with them in an out-of-office environment. After that, then I said 'okay, I'm okay. I can go home now. And that's okay. That's okay.' But I am not sure...But I heard I discussed it with them after that, and they said, 'No, it's perfectly fine.' I mean, it's just it's brave to discuss it as well. I don't want them to see me as snobbish... (Josie, Firefly).

Josie identifies her own introverted nature but bravely attends the function for a short while, worrying that when she leaves early it will be seen as 'snobbish'. She brings it up at work the following week at work and her colleagues reassure that this is 'fine' but she still seems worried about her own non-participation and how it is perceived. This highlights one of the dangers of an enthusiastic and openly 'fun company' where workers can feel that their career may be influenced by their participation—or non-participation in fun activities that make them uncomfortable. When People and Culture leaders in organisations ask me about creating and promoting fun activities (and I have found that fun does concern HRM and People and Culture managers) one of my suggested tweaks is that they always offer an 'opt-out' option where workers can choose whether or not to participate with no pressure and no questions asked if a worker does choose to opt out. There is still normative and implied pressure but at least this is a formal recognition that not everyone enjoys all of the activities offered. I also suggest that in larger companies, different groups take turns at organising activities and events—again with the opt-out clause in play. With variety and different organisers there may be some events that quieter, more introverted workers can enjoy. While all of this is pertinent to in-office fun, the increase in hybrid work has brought changes in fun experiences and perhaps online forms of fun offer quieter, alternative opportunities and a less-worrisome way of opting out which may feel more comfortable for workers online than in face-to-face activities.

Fun Experiences in Hybrid Work

As my research project was focused on fun and well-being at work, and my companies permitted hybrid work, I began to investigate how fun operated when work was both remote/online and in-person. Additionally, in discussions before my most recent research project began, both companies declared that they were 'fun companies' and both identified their 'fun culture' where they emphasised the importance of fun at work. I was keen to find out if fun only happened during in-person interactions or were there other ways that workers expressed their fun side and enjoyed some social interaction even when not in the office? I asked questions of all the staff, including senior managers, and here are some of their responses:

> The design team they, they schedule like a little design hangout at the end of the day. We started it this week, so we - yesterday we did a little Pictionary kind of Zoom vibe, it was really fun. You still get that sense of belonging and that you can hang out with people. That's so much fun, eh? And just the fact that we're doing like picture of the day on Slack and getting people involved. It's so much fun, yeah (Fiona, Gecko).

It seems that Fiona's team has found some creative ways to enjoy fun creating 'hangouts' and Pictionary games as well as sharing pictures on Slack. As I was part of the Slack channel during my time at Gecko I saw many of these pictures which included emojis, some images that had been sourced from the internet, memes, and workers' own photos. Fiona identifies that these fun activities foster 'belonging' in her team. Here are some further thoughts on how fun is experienced in hybrid work:

> I think we want to get used to the new awkward. ... people talking when the microphone's muted, cats walking across screens and things like that. But it is all just part of the fun. I think it's just a - sort of a re-acclimatisation that we just all have to go through (Dev, Gecko founder).

> Fun - I think not a lot at the moment. But what we're trying to do is, you know, we have to bring it in and over the past three months performance, we've done the sort of monthly team meetings where we get together, we have a bit of a quiz at the end of it and that type of thing. But we have a fun committee… (Andy, Firefly, People and Culture Team).

> I think the fact that this team loves connection, and whether they're young or they're just young at heart, they - the connection factor, and the being together and having fun is so important to them (Rose, Firefly, Senior Manager).

These three senior managers recognise the importance of fun in their companies and Dev highlights the awkward aspects of online meetings but suggests these are part of the fun, while Andy alludes to a fun committee and the creation of quizzes as a form of online fun. I do note that quizzes were a very prevalent form of fun during Covid lockdown times and that quizzes were still used regularly after lockdowns. Quizzes are often promoted as a fun way to foster team-building, increase morale, and enhance work engagement but I do truly think that you can have too much of a good thing and sometimes at the end of a long work day feeling that you must join in with a fun quiz, can be irritating and almost a final work task to be completed—extending work hours. Short and sweet and embedded within the workday may be a useful way to incorporate quizzes, while other activities should also be considered especially if a fun committee is formed. If quizzes are a good option for your workplace there are many freely available online and they include trivia games and can be customised to your team needs. As Rose points out above, connection is important and fun, and games can be an important factor in maintaining connection in work teams.

The workers below were not fully convinced about the value of online quizzes and Priya felt that activities like this were more fun when in-person and were useful for bonding. Dana mentions the value of a chat before starting working together -which is easily achieved both online and in office-based meetings and collaboration.

> [sometimes] we do online quizzes which are definitely more fun in the office… And I feel like that sometimes, like, it's still fun … being able to socialise with the people you work with and not just have it be focused like not every interaction, just focused on solely work. That's quite nice, just helps you bond and, you know (Priya, Gecko).

So, all of our fun and enjoyment has been done online. That's really interesting. So, when we come together as a team, it's merged. Usually, the best parts are just the quick chat beforehand where everyone's just checking in carrying (Dana, Gecko).

I was lucky enough to also be permitted access to some online platforms such as Slack where quiz nights were hosted and staff used Slack to talk to each other in a casual light-hearted way. Chat on the Slack channel saw work conversations interspersed with messages that were fun, funny, and light-hearted and this stimulated social interaction and personal enjoyment for some workers.

In this next example I observed and participated in an in-person, office-based game involving the Gecko workers' lanyards. The game had been created by management with the aim of getting all staff to wear their lanyards in the office. If someone was not wearing their lanyard or had left it on their desk, colleagues could snap a photo and submit it to the newly created game site to earn points. Staff caught not wearing their lanyard had points deducted while those that caught them out gained points. Extra points were offered for snapping photos of senior managers without their lanyards. A week after the game started, workers were forced to work from home during a Covid lockdown. During an online chat on Slack, Daisy (receptionist and admin assistant) sent this message (below) to reassure everyone that she was available to help with any admin and work needs. She included a dog emoji and a photo of her own dog wearing her workplace lanyard. Her colleagues were quick to respond, and the original in-person game was spontaneously reinvented (by the youngest employee) and quickly became an online game. Many company members joined the game and prizes were offered. The photos caused a lot of merriment indicated mostly by laughing emojis and cheerful comments. Chocolate was couriered to the winner who snapped a photo of a cow wearing their lanyard! Here is the online chat thread that launched the new photo game:

> 'Hope you are all doing well in your first morning back in our new normal for the next 7 days. Even though we are not in the office just wanted to send a message and let you all know I'm still here as your front desk/ office queen/go to! Flick me a message if you need anything and I'll do my best, OR if you need a break between meetings/work and need some water cooler chat - I'm here. As seen below I also have my assistant ready

for the day to help out 🐶 (emoji as seen here - plus a photo of her dog wearing her lanyard - photo not shown for privacy reasons) (Daisy, Receptionist).

'I think you may have inadvertently started a new lockdown game Daisy - photos of animals wearing GECKO lanyards! Chocolate prize to the most votes at the end of lockdown! GO!!' (Angel, Marketing Manager).

'I like this game a lot' (Marnie, People and Culture Manager).

As I was immersed in the company at the time and participating in the Slack channel, I joined the game and here is a photo of my own lovely dog (Bowie) wearing the lanyard that the Gecko company issued me for the duration of my research visit. I didn't win the game, who can beat a lanyard-wearing cow? But I did have fun and joining the game increased my inclusion in the team while I was in the company. Sharing a photo of my pet felt warm and friendly but also not too personally revealing. In a small side note—for the duration of writing this book Bowie has assumed this comfy position on the couch at my side but is no longer wearing his/my lanyard!

Author's own photo

Although hybrid work can leave some workers feeling disconnected, incorporating fun activities can help to build an inclusive culture that can be maintained online. Fun activities can keep hybrid workers and teams engaged, connected, and motivated, whether they're working remotely or in the office. Activities like online trivia, escape rooms, or hybrid scavenger hunts may help bridge the gap between remote and in-office employees with workers free to simply join or disconnect with activities depending on their interests, workload, and level of well-being. Some companies organise virtual or in-person coffee breaks to foster informal conversations that can strengthen work relationships, similar to in-person coffee breaks in offices. It is even possible to organise events such as virtual happy hours or hybrid game nights that allow both remote and in-office employees to participate. Flexible fun breaks can be a good idea to encourage workers to take short breaks for relaxation, and these may include a quick walk—maybe sharing a nature photo with the team, a fun online challenge, the ever-popular quizzes, riddles, or a virtual meditation session. Interactive tools such as virtual whiteboards or hybrid brainstorming sessions can make work tasks more fun and engaging, and increasingly there are interesting creative options for hybrid meetings and interactions.

Hybrid Fun Enhances Happiness

While there are current studies on the impacts of fun at work, very few address fun in relation to hybrid work. With my research partner, Dr Rhiannon Lloyd, we have contributed two recent studies on fun in hybrid work (Plester & Lloyd, 2023, 2024). One of these identified that in the right conditions, when workers feel safe to express themselves in an authentic way, then fun enhances their workplace well-being and happiness. From our research findings, our suggestion was that managers and workers can collaborate to encourage new forms of fun that blend online activities with in-person fun but still try to maintain spontaneity in fun. Although this sounds complicated, the example above where the in-office game was modified to become an online activity exemplifies how this might occur and we noted that sometimes younger workers such as Daisy, have strengths in online interaction that might be employed creatively towards fun activities. Workers with online expertise such as the digital natives, might be enthused to help design games, activities, or ways of expressing fun, humour, and pleasure that can occur in-person while also adapting activities into innovative online options. This may have the added benefit of creating greater inclusion and highlighting skills of younger workers as evidenced when the marketing and people and culture managers quickly saw the potential in Daisy' spontaneous pet-lanyard post. After the lanyard game concluded and a prize had been awarded, the Gecko company created several follow-up online photo challenges during the lockdown period and these were popular with many workers joining in, including senior leaders. The key to keeping and fostering as much fun as possible may be to embrace a variety of different forms, retaining some in-person activities and spontaneous fun occurrences, while also generating online opportunities and most importantly allowing workers to opt in or out as they choose. Certainly, online fun is gaining more popularity and momentum as companies embrace gamification for a variety of well-being and performance benefits.

Gamification

A popular way to promote engagement and connectivity in hybrid work teams is through gamification. Gamification is a term that has been around since 2003 where games or game-like elements are applied to non-game contexts with the aim of enhancing motivation and having some workplace fun to enhance engagement and motivation (Dale, 2014) There are usually a range of rewards for users that exhibit the right behaviours and rewards may include points, badges, and leaderboards, depending on the game. Gamification is commonly used in workplaces for education, marketing, and even fitness apps may be gamified to encourage participation and improve performance and well-being. Gamification can be useful and enjoyable in workplace education and development programmes (Coelho & Abreu, 2023).

Gamification seems to consider both workers' performance and their mental health, even helping people feel better in their jobs, while also allowing some company control and improved performance that may boost company gains. Gamification may be an attractive way for companies to engage a range of employees, particularly younger workers who are digital natives. Finding a balance of gaming that creates enjoyment while achieving work goals and boosting performance may be the key to gamification. As gamification lends itself to online activities, this may be a beneficial way of fostering enjoyment and connection in hybrid teams especially with published results, rewards, and some exciting prizes offered. It requires some creativity and development, or gamification tools can be purchased from software solution sites such as Gametize, Funifier and Mambo to name a few.

LEGO® Serious Play® (LSP) is an example of gamification where building and creating using LEGO bricks as a means of expression is a game-based method designed to unlock creativity, foster collaboration, and deepen understanding. However, as already discussed in this chapter, using fun and gamification does not engage or excite everyone and Dana (below) is unconvinced of its merits:

> And I sat through a LEGO® Serious Play®. Oh, yes. And it was just awful but the way they tried to try and tie it back to how you're creating strategy is a loose, loose connection.... And this is what we're trying to achieve as a team that sort of strategic element to it doesn't work with Lego play. So, I think we don't get it right. And I think that's the thing is it. Fun is not the same for everyone. So, I think there needs to be options (Dana, Firefly).

Turning Tasks into Play: Gamification Ideas

Team challenges involving both remote and in-person collaboration can be designed and can involve work targets such as sales numbers or can involve light-hearted challenges such as spotting errors or mistakes on websites or shared documents. Virtual leaderboards can be created and published where friendly competition is encouraged by tracking achievements from remote and in-office employees. Gamified training modules with interactive learning and quizzes, badges, and progress tracking can be developed or purchased from software suppliers. Recognition and rewards are a popular part of gamification where achievements or wins can be celebrated and published with digital badges, shoutouts, or incentives. I observed this in Gecko where workers used the Slack channel to give a weekly 'shout out' to someone that had achieved something big or even just a quite small act that was noticed by a colleague and chocolate bars were proffered as rewards.

Hybrid scavenger hunts are becoming popular as they engage workers with online and offline activities creating blended participation. They can be creative and fun and can be themed with a list of items to find, or challenges to complete—either online, in the office and environs, or across a mixture of both workspaces. They may include clues involving riddles or prompts with points awarded for completed items or tasks. There is usually a time limit, and the hunt can be conducted individually or in teams—teams are particularly useful in hybrid work as some members can complete online challenges while others undertake the in-person tasks depending on where teammates are working. There needs to be clear communication channels and tech support for collaboration between team members. Examples of this are photo or video challenges, puzzles or riddles, finding information on specific websites, outdoor walks finding natural items and these can be completed from home or the office with actual items displayed or photographic evidence uploaded from remote workers. The only limits are safety, and the creativity of tasks assigned. Ideas can be sourced from multiple websites such as Outback Team Building and Team Building Hub, most of which offer hybrid options. See for example: 17 Scavenger Hunt Team Building Activities for Workgroups Virtual Scavenger Hunts: 25 Ideas for Team Building (https://www.outbackteambuilding.com/blog/scavenger-hunt-team-building-activities/).

Gamification can be fun, creative, and a powerful tool for engagement and performance improvement, but it does create some potential issues. For example, games can become fierce through excessive competition, and overemphasising leaderboards and rankings can increase stress and may even result in a toxic work environment. Thus, care must be taken to keep games light and fun. Motivation is complex and overusing gamification may create a reliance on external rewards that diminishes finding fulfilment in other aspects of work. There may be privacy issues to consider if games are tracking worker behaviour or requiring photos taken of personal situations or items, and data security may also be a consideration—even in games. As noted in my early research, fun activities can be a distraction from actual work tasks and if workers get too involved, getting them to refocus on other work objectives may be a challenge. Poorly designed games can feel exploitative and for some employees may feel too child-like or silly. Games may even be used as an insidious form of workplace control to boost company results (Coelho & Abreu, 2023) and be presented as a boost to happiness and well-being while sometimes not achieving that at all. Gamification is an option to be used cautiously and researched fully for options that truly fit your work team and company style.

Fun Rules

While there are no rules to fun and no one wants to be accused of being the 'fun police', understanding the complexity of fun and how people experience it is important when organising fun activities or events. It is hard to plan fun experiences that please everyone because everyone's idea of fun is individual. Added to this, some people just do not want to engage in fun at work, so a takeaway point (as discussed above), is always have an opt-out option so that people are not coerced into enduring a fun activity that they find unpleasant or demeaning.

Overall fun can be experienced as an enjoyable and a happy time at work, but hybrid work offers both new challenges and opportunities for fun moments. The companies that I researched were highly motivated to ensure that they still had fun when some workers were online and some in the office, so they tried to create blended fun where some events occurred in-person, others were hosted online, and some traversed between both formats. The key to this is balance and sensitivity and understanding the people you work with, as well as doing some homework to find options that might work both in remote and in-office work. I gave some examples of this and conclude by noting that gamification is an increasingly popular way to promote fun, competition, and some good-natured social work-based activity. The enjoyment of fun in modern workplaces is changing in response to hybrid and remote forms of work and therefore is a focus for People and Culture teams—especially those that pride themselves on maintaining a 'fun culture'—the topic of Chapter 3.

References

Burawoy, M. (1979). *Manufacturing consent. Changes in the labour process under monopoly capitalism*. University of Chicago Press.

Coelho, F., & Abreu, A. M. (2023). The Corporate (Magic) Circle: Fun Work or Controlled Play? *Tech Trends, 67*(1), 160–177.

Dale, S. (2014). Gamification: Making work fun or making fun of work? *Business Information Review, 31*(2), 82–90.

Fleming, P. (2005). Worker's playtime? Boundaries and cynicism in a 'Culture of fun' program. *The Journal of Applied Behavioral Science, 41*(3), 285–303.

Plester, B.A. (2009). Crossing the line: Boundaries of workplace humour and fun. *Employee Relations, 31*(6), 584–599.

Plester, B., & Lloyd, R. (2024). New frontiers of fun: Sharing and supporting workplace fun in hybrid work. *Employee Relations: THe International Journal, 46*(4), 934–954.

Plester, B. A., & Lloyd, R. (2023). Happiness Is 'Being Yourself': Psychological Safety and Fun in Hybrid Work. *Administrative Sciences, 13*(10), 218.

Roy, D. (1959). 'Banana Time': Job satisfaction and informal interaction. *Human Organisation Studies, 18,* 158–168.

Tews, M. J., Michel, J. W., & Allen, D. G. (2014). Fun and friends: The impact of workplace fun and constituent attachment on turnover in a hospitality context. *Human Relations, 67*(8), 923–946. https://doi.org/10.1177/0018726713508143

How to Have Fun at Work with Employees: 20 Ideas. Retrieved March 21, 2025, from https://teambuilding.com/blog/fun-at-work

26 Best Virtual Team Celebration Ideas for Work. Retrieved March 21, 2025, from https://teambuilding.com/blog/virtual-team-celebration

50 Fun Activities to Boost Engagement with Remote and Hybrid Teams. Retrieved March 21, 2025, from https://www.hrmorning.com/wp-content/uploads/2022/05/50-Fun-Activities-to-Boost-Engagement-with-Remote-and-Hybrid-Teams_Preciate.pdf

Gametize | Enterprise Gamification & White-label Platform. Retrieved March 21, 2025, from https://start.gametize.com/

Funifier | Gamification Solutions. Retrieved March 21, 2025, from https://www.funifier.com/

Mambo Enterprise Gamification Platform—On-Premise and SaaS Software. Retrieved March 21, 2025, from https://mambo.io/

17 Scavenger Hunt Team Building Activities for Workgroups. Retrieved March 21, 2025, from https://www.outbackteambuilding.com/blog/scavenger-hunt-team-building-activities/

Virtual Scavenger Hunts: 25 Ideas for Team Building. Retrieved March 21, 2025, from https://teambuildinghub.com/team-building/virtual/activities-games/scavenger-hunts/

CHAPTER 3

Fun Reimagined: People and Culture in the Hybrid Workplace

Organisational Culture and Climate

Emerging from different academic traditions, both organisational culture and climate are complex, overlapping constructs that are not easily defined, although there is a key difference in how they are usually researched. Studies of organisational climate tend to use statistical analyses of individual attitudes and perceptions of the organisational atmosphere. Climate studies explore the 'mood' created in the workplace and investigate how workers feel about their organisation (Al-Shammari, 1992). Alternatively, organisational culture is a shared concept where company norms are developed that influence key aspects such as behaviour, performance, and worker engagement. Culture is more often ethnographically studied (Hoy, 2010) through immersion and engagement with the organisation and this is the approach that I use in all of my research. Therefore, my research is mostly underpinned using the collective concept of organisational culture, but I acknowledge that climate is also important, and both concepts are relevant to how workplace dynamics are perceived and understood.

Organisational culture includes the many aspects of an organisation that members value, believe in, and prioritise. It can include, but it is not limited to, values, attitudes, systems, rules, norms, mission statements, and beliefs and these features influence the behaviours of people in the organisation. While parts of organisational culture may be made

© The Author(s), under exclusive license to Springer Nature Singapore Pte Ltd. 2025
B. Plester, *Hybrid Happiness*,
https://doi.org/10.1007/978-981-95-2092-3_3

explicit such as a mission statement or articulation of company values, there are deep underlying aspects that are implicit and assumed (Schein, 1985, 2004). Over time, socialised company members come to know and understand these deeply embedded aspects of organisational culture that are sometimes called 'assumptions' in research models (see Schein, 1985, 2004). Organisational culture comprised of complex, entangled features such as norms, artefacts, values, and assumptions can be a powerful determinant of peoples' workplace behaviour. Organisational culture can be likened to an iceberg with some of it visible and apparent (maybe a third) with many aspects below the sightline and assumed and implicitly understood.

Organisational culture may become entwined with the organisational brand which can influence marketing aspects and reflect how the organisation sees itself. For example, I have worked with companies that market themselves as a 'fun company' in order to recruit and retain talented employees. In organisations that establish and develop a strong culture, people may identify closely with the culture and perceive a shared organisational identity that they reference and portray to stakeholders both within and outside the business. In some of the companies that I have studied a fun culture is readily viewed as a positive and brand-worthy identity by most, if not all, organisational members. Organisational culture is usually experienced as a shared or collective phenomenon with key features that most organisational members agree upon while still retaining individual perceptions and interpretations. It has a focus upon characteristics such as beliefs, symbols, narratives, language, myths, stories, rituals and how these are transmitted in an organisation especially during socialisation into a company (Trice & Beyer, 1993). Culture is tricky to assess and understand and this is why I adopt my personal research approach of full immersion as this allows me to appreciate culture in depth, moving beyond the surface levels of artefacts and articulated values and gleaning deeper insights into the underlying assumptions that permeate the organisation and its culture.

Organisational climate is a similar related and overlapping concept that refers to a worker's perception over time of the organisation and culture. It is a more feelings-based concept concerned with atmosphere, attitudes, leadership style, and morale (Schneider et al., 2011). I will use the notion of climate more extensively in Chapter 4 where I discuss psychologically safe climates (PSC) and the impact of these on humour and fun. Climate may be experienced and interpreted differently depending on personality traits and is considered to be a more individual concept than organisational culture which focuses upon shared ideals and behavioural norms. Climate is loosely related to the atmosphere or mood in an organisation and the meaning that people attach to their workplace experiences. The concept of climate tends to have a shorter-term focus as it may be more changeable in response to events and may fluctuate more readily than culture which has a longer-term residency. Climate reflects the mood of the organisation whereas culture displays its personality or identity. Climate is seen as easier to measure and there are surveys that assess this and these include measurement of employee attitudes and feelings, sometimes assessed in tools such as engagement surveys or other similar assessment tools.

While entire books have been written on these two entwined yet differentiated concepts, the focus here is on how these concepts influence humour and fun at work. Culture and/or climate can determine the types of fun and humour that are shared, can create restraints to humour and fun by determining what is forbidden, and can dictate policies and protocols for Human Resources or People and Culture teams. The increasing uptake of hybrid work adds a further layer of complexity as social interaction involving humour and fun may be shared in-person, online, or via a blend of both mediums simultaneously and asynchronously. The changes to work modes due to more remote work and hybrid work models is influencing organisational culture and climate and in turn, having an impact on fun and humour interactions in this blended environment. This has repercussions for employee well-being and happiness and thus has been the focus of my most recent research. Now that I have briefly established some key aspects of organisational culture and climate theories, I introduce two companies working in hybrid mode and illustrate how this has changed their climate and culture and subsequently influenced their workplace fun and humour interactions.

Two Fun Companies

Am important aspect of collecting data on people and organisations is respect and care for all participants, and I believe that this especially important in the ethnographic, immersive approach that I use within companies. Care is also demanded by university ethics boards who have stringent rules about confidentiality, anonymity, and respect for participants. Therefore, I note that all names used in discussing specific examples are pseudonyms- for companies, individuals, teams, and divisions within these workplaces. At times I even have to change or omit some key details of a company or a team if specific details might compromise their confidentiality. However, for the most part details are correct, changes are only to names, and all quoted extracts are verbatim quotes. Descriptions of companies are as close as I can get them without compromising confidentiality and I will briefly describe the two companies with the conferred pseudonyms of Gecko and Firefly.

Gecko

As a digital design and technology company Gecko thrives on creating innovative solutions that can enhance people's lives. They have operated for 16 years; the company is privately owned and has a workforce of 70 led by a board of shareholders. The founder and CEO highly value the company culture which they see as vibrant, fun, and dynamic. When I arrived at Gecko, they had recently formalised their policy for hybrid work allowing their employees to work in the office and at home, or from a remote location. Employees are able to establish their own personalised work rhythm that can support their family needs and lifestyle preferences. Most employees work either two or three days at home, coming into the office for the other days, although this may vary depending on their work demands. Tuesdays have been designated as 'all staff' days where everyone is expected to come into the office in-person by 9am for a company-wide meeting.

All of the Gecko staff define their workplace as a 'fun company' and emphasize that this is an important cultural attribute. The contemporary, open-plan office has an industrial-inspired design with exposed ductwork and central open spaces which supports their collaborative teamwork. Small, vividly coloured enclosed meeting rooms surround the open floor, and these are used for client or team meetings, reserved through a central booking system. The office space includes (fun) recreational equipment including a table tennis table, netball hoop, juke box, popcorn machine and a sophisticated industrial-grade coffee machine is provided for all-day coffee in the kitchen. Free fruit and soft drinks are supplied weekly. In break areas there are games, puzzles, and a guitar provided for staff enjoyment and relaxation. The popcorn maker in the kitchen is a popular artefact and the tantalising aromas entice staff to congregate in the kitchen area for chats, snacks, and laughter.

Gecko also has a pet-friendly policy and during the time I was there, different dogs visited and wandered through the office for pats and affection. This employee privilege was restricted to one dog (I never saw any other type of pet) per day to avoid canine chaos and an employee's pet visit must be pre-booked via the People and Culture manager. Displayed on the walls throughout the office are inspiring mottos, essential security reminders, and company values. Workflows are mostly informal, and I observed joking, swearing, and laughter throughout most days. No-one occupies a fixed workstation, and so workers choose their daily workspace according to their needs or inclinations each day. This informal space allocation inspires relaxed interactions, is ever-changing, and generates playfulness, interaction, and useful collaboration. Employees claimed to like this casual set-up, and it reflects their collaborative yet relaxed organisational style and culture.

Firefly

A sizeable food manufacturing organisation, Firefly has a large workforce exceeding 600 staff including permanent employees and contractors. They operate a busy factory with 300 workers that daily work in three, eight-hour shifts. Supporting the manufacturing operation are multiple office-based teams. I was hosted by two different office teams, one being the Research and Development (R&D) team and the second was the People and Culture team responsible for HR processes and communication and well-being processes. These two teams were located in different buildings and traversing between them required following a specific safe pathway wearing a high visibility jacket. Both office buildings displayed brightly painted slogans and logos that were playful, vibrant, and a reflection of the company focus on fun at work. Office space in both team locations was bright, with a variety of decorations including party lights and photographs throughout. These decorations and displays increased over the Christmas season and I was lucky to be situated at Firefly during this festive time. There were also extra team celebrations and parties over the Christmas season, although not all employees celebrated or observed the Christmas festival.

Similar to Gecko, Firefly also operates a hybrid work model where office employees can work from home, generally for two days and for the remining three days employees attend work on-site. This policy is flexible, and some employees can work from home (or remotely) for three days with the expectation of least two days on-site. The office-based teams nominate one 'Anchor Day' usually mid-week where all employees are expected to attend meetings and in-person collaboration. Firefly has implemented a formal policy for hybrid work for office workers, but this is not an option for factory workers who work shifts. My observations showed that most office-based staff chose to work remotely on Mondays and Fridays making Tuesdays, Wednesdays and Thursdays the busy in-person office days. Staff were enthusiastic about this flexible work pattern with many employees describing the benefits of this fluid arrangement and the positive impact upon their well-being due to the balance they could achieve between home and work life. They also noted some of the disadvantages to hybrid work and these are discussed later in the book.

Employees at Firefly considered workplace fun to be a significant value in the company and this was enthusiastically endorsed by both managers and lower-level workers. There was the suggestion that at times there was too much fun, but this aspect is more fully explored in the following sections.

HUMOUR, FUN, AND PLAY. WHAT'S THE DIFFERENCE?

When talking to people at work about humour or fun they use the terms interchangeably. Often, they also bring in the term 'play' or talk about being 'playful' at work. While this terminological overlap is not an issue for them and I can always ask them further questions to really understand what they are saying, it does cause issues for me when I write about these three concepts. As I do academic work, I must rest my theorisation and scholarly papers on fairly precise theory. It is easy to simply segue between all of these concepts and treat them as the same thing, but I try to be more specific than that in my research work. For clarity, I will briefly differentiate them here while also pointing out the overlap between each concept. I will attempt to use each term in the correct way but as I present verbatim extracts from my participants, I have noted that sometimes they answer a question about humour by talking about fun (or vice versa) and also bring in the idea of play and playfulness when discussing their thoughts on these topics. As I value these verbatim extracts, I have to simply accept the terminological fluidity. Research participants also bring in the notion of happiness, but that is more fully discussed in Chapters 1 and 6. Therefore, while I will briefly define all three here so that the nuanced differences are apparent, I am going to allow myself (and my participants) some fluidity between concepts but will at least start from this defined position.

Fun

The project whereby I collected data for this book has its' focus on fun at work and what fun means for employee well-being. While I did not specifically ask people about happiness, they often referred to this concept and included it as part of their thinking about fun and well-being. Fun is considered to be light-hearted, enjoyable, amusing and the notion of pleasure is embedded in the fun concept. Fun can be playful but can also be experienced while doing something serious such as a work task. For example, I encountered people who considered working with spreadsheets to be fun (for them) while for me spreadsheets are usually my least favourite work task, thus not fun at all! This shows that the concept of fun is held in a very individual way among different people depending on likes, dislikes, personality, and a diverse range of personal factors. Of course, fun may create humour and laughter, and it is often likely to cause these reactions, but this is not an essential part of fun. In short—fun does not have to be *funny*— but it can be.

Humour

Humour is a more complicated construct than fun and many of the ancient philosophers such as Socrates, Plato, Hobbes, and Aristotle debated humour and laughter. Humour is (usually) intended to be amusing, funny, and evoke laughter. It includes the comical and humour can be absurd or even ludicrous. Where humour and fun are markedly different is that humour might **not** be light-hearted or even enjoyable. Something can be funny to some people and really unpleasant to others. Both Plato and Aristotle argued that humour is immoral as it can be cruel towards someone targeted in a joke. Humour is complex because it can be funny and unkind at the same time. Some humour works like that. Take for example an ethnic joke that is aimed at, and mocks, a particular group of people. While some people may find this funny and laugh, those that are the target of the joke can be highly upset and offended, or others might be offended on their behalf. It is possible to be both offended and amused simultaneously, which can be confusing. Humour can contain a message or a barb if it is aimed and targeted. As far back as 1905, Freud identified that using 'joke-work' or humour may allow a person to say the 'unsayable', where they express ideas that are not really socially acceptable. Freud linked this to sex and aggression, topics that might not be discussed openly, but may be revealed in joking interactions.

Dark topics or jocular insults are just one way that humour might work. Of course, it may also create merriment, inclusion, and camaraderie when a group all enjoy the same joke or humorous interaction but there is often the potential for humour to be misconstrued and cause dissonance. Dating back to medieval times, humour was considered to be a state of mind (the four humours were part of medical diagnoses) and so we sometimes refer to a person as being of, or in, 'good humour'. While there is overlap with fun, and some humour is a part of fun and caused by fun, there are types of humour that a have dark side and this separates it distinctly from the pleasant, lightness of fun.

Play

Workplace play is defined as both a diversion from workplace tasks as well as a way of engaging with them and play is sometimes fostered as a way of increasing creativity and innovation at work. Play has an active component so is usually defined as activity-based, differing from humour and fun. Some humour and fun may be solely verbal exchanges and while these may be *playful*, they are not considered as play per se. The research on this topic (Celestine & Yeo, 2021) suggests that organisational (work) play is quite strategic, such as a task presented as a game to make it more appealing. Play can be used in workplace schemes such as LEGO® SERIOUS PLAY® to increase innovation and creative thinking. Workplace play does convey some of the same lightness that the fun concept invokes but playing games can be highly competitive (especially at work) and for some people this may reduce the pleasure aspect, while for others this increases pleasure. Play does not necessarily include humour, although it can, and play includes a wide range of activities including sports, virtual games, hobbies and even toys. Using play at work is increasing in popularity and hybrid work has helped initiate a plethora of online play activities such as quizzes, games, and competitions with new activities constantly emerging.

A Fun Framework

As the key focus of my recent research was upon fun and well-being, here I will briefly explain a typology of fun that I developed with two psychology colleagues some years ago, but that is still being used and cited in fun studies (Plester et al., 2015). The reason I'm presenting this is that these three types of workplace fun have a strong relationship with workplace culture and managerial processes within companies and it helps explain some of the participant's reactions to changes in workplace fun when working in a hybrid format.

Managed Fun

In all of my research on fun spanning twenty years, I have found that 'managed fun' is the least popular form of workplace fun. Managed fun is defined as workplace fun at that is generated and promoted (usually but not always) by managers such as those responsible for well-being or it may be organised by managers/members of the People and Culture team. The Gecko company even had 'culture champions' responsible for organising fun events, celebrations, and enjoyable activities. While many managed fun initiatives are enjoyable and popular there is also the **forced** aspect of this type of fun whereby company members feel that they have to participate in the fun to be a 'team player' or to show their lighter side and their personality. Many people are uncomfortable with this dynamic. Also, sometimes leaving work aside to have fun can be onerous as people may be really busy and so fun draws them away from crucial work tasks and this can be experienced as stressful or distracting. Some workers simply prefer to complete work tasks during work times and leave fun until they are away from work in their own leisure time. Because fun is specific to individual worker's likes and preferences, work-created fun may not be considered to be fun by everyone as described in the example from Chapter 2 where everyone was encouraged to dress up as a TV or movie character and one worker found this so confronting that he stayed home! (in Plester & Hutchison, 2016).

Organic Fun

Throughout my research, organic fun has emerged as the most popular type of fun experienced at work. This type of fun simply happens naturally and spontaneously. It does not feel forced, and people enjoy the authenticity encapsulated in this kind of fun. This type of fun is strongly related to organisational culture where the conditions for fun are ideal, and workers and managers are comfortable in enjoying moments of fun throughout their workday. These types of organisations often pride themselves on their fun culture where fun is simply a natural (organic) part of the workday. Happily, I have seen lots of organic fun during my times within companies and this type of fun varies from small micro-moments of fun such as throwing a squishy ball at a colleague, to bigger activities that occur spontaneously, such as one time in a company when I observed a food fight spontaneously erupt in the open plan office space (Note: there are quite a few cultural issues with this incident but they have been analysed in an earlier book (see Plester, 2016).

Task Fun

I've already referred to task fun where someone enjoys specific tasks of their work and they experience work tasks as a type of fun (remember the spreadsheets?). Some people get so absorbed in their tasks that they not only experience fun, but they move into the state of 'flow' (Csikszentmihalyi et al., 2014) that becomes total absorption. Throughout my years of research, many participants have expressed enjoyment in this flow state and consider it to be a type of fun as it gives them pleasure while they are totally and happily absorbed in the task.

Work has changed for many people and now more work is conducted online within offices as well as from remote locations such as workers' homes or cafes. Work teams are not always co-located and may operate from different locations around the world. As workers still place significant importance on having workplace fun this has resulted in new forms of online fun that are sometimes embedded within work tasks, and this constitutes 'task fun' in the fun typology. For example, sometimes work tasks are made into games such as quizzes or other competitive online tasks that are partly work and partly fun (and a form of play). This happened in my own workplace recently where a specific team wanted staff to learn some important information. They presented it as a quiz and although people were present in a meeting room, it was conducted online using a QR code accessed by a device. More than 80 staff joined simultaneously and answered questions using their smart phones. It was a work task but the gamification of it made it fun—causing chatter and laughter as everyone strove to be the top player. Many of my research participants told similar stories of quizzes and games when working online or with global teams, and I even joined some online quizzes and games when working with Gecko and Firefly. This aspect of having fun both online and in person (or both) is impacting and changing organisational culture.

Fun and Flexibility

Hybrid work is a flexible work arrangement where employees can work in the physical office and in remote locations, usually their home, or sometimes other off-site locations. This allows workers to balance their life commitments with their work ones. Hybrid work allows for some in-office collaboration alongside the flexibility of remote work. Although many companies have offered hybrid work options for several years the uptake of hybrid arrangements was escalated by the Covid pandemic and hybrid work has been sustained globally post-Covid.

Hybrid work has been a game-changer for many workers because it brings lots of novel benefits as well as some challenging effects for workplaces. For example, one challenge is that it can make workers feel alone and detached and they may miss face-to-face social interaction such as office-based fun (Ghosh et al., 2023). Some workers have lamented the loss of sensory encounters such as shared food and drink, physical interactions, and non-verbal communication (Stanko et al., 2022). Such losses are offset by the convenience of less time lost during commuting, ease of family care arrangements (including pet care), and the proximity to local services. Most of my participants from both Gecko and Firefly discussed their fun culture in regard to flexibility and Angel particularly notes some of the office-based features that help create the fun culture in her workplace, while Rose notes the benefits of fun that apply at Firefly:

> I spend more time with my kids now [since Covid]. And I know that they're welcome here [at Gecko premises] if required and they think it's cool. They're, like, wow, you've got an office with a popcorn machine, that's so cool. I want them to think my workplace is cool. I want them to have the opinion that, you know, what I do for a job is cool, that tech is

> cool. And also, to be exposed to that very diverse multi-gendered, multi-ethnicity workplace. We always, like, share cool, like, stickers and stuff so that's, you know, we'll talk about that. There are people who, I like to talk to about music. There are people who, you could just, like, rock up to their desk and just be, like, what's going on? So, for me the relationships are the most fun thing about it, yeah… I had a giggle when I walked in this morning and saw the netball hoop up. And my, like, awful mum voice kicked in it was, like, 'that ball's going to bounce, make noise. Going to knock a computer off someone's desk'. I'm going to stand up and say, 'don't play inside the house with the ball'…I do have a lot of fun (Angel, Marketing Manager Gecko).

> It's a work-hard/ play-hard team. It's not like, yeah, it's not like they're just doing fun stuff all the time and get nothing done. They work real hard. And I think what it does is when you have a bit of fun, it kind of allows you to breathe. And it allows you to sort of sit back from just the intensity of it all. And I guess maybe there is sort of a centering tone and a reflection and an appreciation and gratitude that comes with it (Rose, Senior Manager, Firefly).

One the biggest challenges noted by participants from both Firefly and Gecko was the change to organisational culture and climate and in particular the reduction and change in social aspects such as events and work celebrations. These participants share their thoughts about culture change caused by hybrid work:

> I think the culture is - is one of people come to work to work hard, but to enjoy themselves. And there's a strong sense of having, wanting to have fun when you're at work… people have probably, well, they've got out of the habit, enjoying work, they got to have the habit of coming to work, and got out of the habit of socialising while at work. Yeah, there are some people that may have started here - that may have been in the office six times. We've lost that opportunity for pulling teams together, and seeing teams grow together. And building that sense of sort of psychological trust in a team that says, we're allowed to have fun, we're allowed to have a crack, break, because we're a team. But it's almost like we're having to start again, as to how do we get that happening? (Andy, Well-being Manager, Firefly).

I spend an hour getting to work and I spend an hour coming back from work. But the time that I spend at work, that cross pollination, of information, of sharing of knowledge of getting to know people and developing relationships that's lost in that hybrid environment, because as you say, I'm on a zoom call. I'm all for zoom calls. There are no niceties. There's no getting to know somebody, it's all business, right (Phil[1], 56, Food technologist).

I like social activities, so having to do that over video phone is an okay substitute, but it's just not like the same thing… I think we want to get used to the new awkward. … People talking when the microphone's muted, cats walking across, friends and things like that. But it is all just part of the fun. I think it's just a sort of a re-acclimatisation that we just all have to go through (Dev, Founder, Gecko).

I would say it's always a little bit, feels a bit more forced. So, virtual, like, sort of, like, virtual meetings or virtual catch ups it's not as organic or as in the moment. Which generally is, sort of, what you, where the true moments of fun and kind of, like, joy come from is kind of spur of the moment stuff (Jack, Gecko).

I think the hard thing is in the virtual world. You find yourself maybe writing stuff down. And if you think about the language, right? I mean, when you see someone, when you hear what they say, and you see their expressions… So, when you so when you have to do lots of email in online stuff, which is often written, yeah, you don't get that? You don't always get - you don't always get the rest of the communication… it has a downside, and it does mean that you have to think more carefully about what you're writing and how that's going to be interpreted… So, we've lost a certain amount of spontaneity (Gail, Firefly).

I also don't really like working from home because it's like kind of hard to switch off at the end of the day. And it's yeah, and it's like no clear boundaries… cause the days that we have to work from the office are Tuesday and then depending on what squad you're in you choose what day you want to come in (Jason, Gecko).

From these extracts we see that culture has changed especially in regard to having fun with colleagues which seems harder to achieve in online

---

[1] This extract from Alexandra's study—see acknowledgements.

work modes. Linking back to the three-part model of fun, Jack has noted that fun is not as organic as it used to be and that it now feels more forced, and Gail notes the loss of spontaneity. Dev talks of the 'new awkward' and Phil makes the point that it is 'all business' in Zoom calls. It seems that people are still making the transition and trying to work out how to still have social interaction and some forms of fun, but that this is not yet a successful part of hybrid work. This has resulted in a loss of some prior fun interactions, somewhat eroding the much-vaunted fun culture in both companies. As I write this the Washington Post is running a story about Amazon enforcing return-to-office policies in order to strengthen culture, foster collaboration, and team connection (April 2024). To offset these cultural changes my research identifies that new online forms of fun are emerging in the use of memes, emojis, quizzes, Zoom chats, and games and this seems likely to be significant in future workplace fun as it evolves and changes.

Hybrid Fun and Games

Even with a loss of some cultural elements and less social interaction, the workers I studied were adamant that they wanted to retain the flexibility of hybrid work. In this next set of extracts, workers and managers clearly articulate the beneficial effects that they feel outweigh some of the challenges and changes experienced in hybrid work. Jasper notes that the flexibility is a key advantage especially when he can avoid rush hour traffic and Angel makes the point that hybrid work was already an option at Gecko but that the Covid pandemic increased the speed at which hybrid options were formalised and taken up by workers.

> I'm able to do hybrid work. I do have a lot that requires me to be here. Um, I like to be here. Four to five days… but I just come in later leave later or work from home for the first part. So, it's all adults. Quite flexible, just strictly about the traffic to be honest, because that's - yeah, tell me about it. It's completely changed how - how people can balance work and life (Jasper, Firefly).

> Who could say whether or not remote working to this degree would have happened had the pandemic not forced it. Familywise, no, I feel like I spend more time with my kids now. I love Slack [online platform used at Gecko], somebody's always sharing a silly meme, something stupid. There's a lot of intelligence within the fun (Angel, Gecko).

While Angel has noted that there is 'intelligent' online fun as well as silly fun, Gail (below) has changed how meetings are run in order to have some fun and social interaction online. Most of her team works remotely and she has seen the importance of strong team connection through chats and shared laughter at the start of meetings.

> I have lots of fun. Online. Yeah, yeah. It's hilarious. So - so we've actually built a really tight connection... we share our personal stories... we never have a meeting where you just get straight to business...one day, I said, 'hey, let's just accept the fact that first five minutes of every meeting, there's time to small talk and vent.' And you know, and, and often it continues throughout the meeting, and we'll have a laugh, and we'll have a chat (Gail, Firefly).

What emerges from everyone in the study is that social interaction and fun has changed in their workplace, but as both companies put a high priority on being a fun company, fun has not disappeared. Rather, fun, humour, and playful interaction is shared in new ways, that are still emerging. Memes, games, quizzes and online chat are replacing traditional water cooler conversations, and many workers are thinking about how best to transfer their light-heartedness into the online forms so that these important stress-relieving aspects are not lost in hybrid work. The changes have affected some of the physical workplace activities that used to prevail, and some traditional play and fun artefacts may no longer be treasured workplace resources.

ARTEFACTS OF FUN: WHAT HAPPENED TO PING PONG?

As hybrid work permits workers to stay at home to complete their tasks, some of the traditional workplace social events and actions have changed due to reduced physical, in-office presence and participation by staff. This presents challenges especially within these two companies that have enthusiastically cultivated and endorsed a fun culture. For example, Firefly has uplifting slogans, bright colours, and shapes painted on walls throughout all of their office buildings. This cultural artefact is designed to make workers feel happy, uplifted, and showcases that Firefly promotes fun and happiness at work. Irene outlines this dynamic:

One of the reasons why I chose to be here is that everybody's quite chill. And the moment I walk into the building, as you can see all these colours, does make you feel happy. It has a very important psychological effect. You know, you see this and then you see fun. And as you see the green house, we have like the set up with all of the you know, fairy lights. And it's beautiful that the balloons was for, like a celebration, but not normally there. But the fairy lights is and all of these colour palettes. I don't know who designed it, but it's brilliant. So it gives you that feeling of energy and fun (Irene, Firefly).

Interestingly, both companies have a table tennis table for staff use. Although it was once a popular activity for fun and a break, the table tennis tables were less frequently used once hybrid work became more prevalent. Jasper reflects that perhaps table tennis is not appropriate in the new hybrid work modes, and this echoes other participants who similarly noted that when they are in the office, they maximise their in-person time with meetings, tasks, and collaboration because this co-located time is now reduced through hybrid work. It seems that playing table tennis, once a thriving enjoyable activity, has fallen out of vogue in the new work mode. Jasper explains this decline while Bao and Gail outline some of the activities that have replaced table tennis:

[We used to have] table tennis out in the hall. I'm still trying to drive that. Because it used to be the thing. You know, like every lunchtime, everybody lining up to get a turn? Yeah, back in the day. And now it's so hard to convince people to play... some of the like, more enthusiastic people have left. Yeah. And there's not enough people who enjoy playing. And then then there's, I don't know, because there's fewer people, everybody might feel like that. This is strictly conjecture - but I think some people might worry that if they're seen playing table tennis, even if it's a lunchtime, because there's fewer people around to make it sort of acceptable. You know, it used to be lots of people in the table tennis area. So, it was like, you know, I don't know what the combined effects... like maybe self-conscious or, or like, you know, worried that it reflects badly (Jasper, Firefly).

So, what are the different ways that you connect? I mean, we often can't play table tennis together anymore. Oh, no. So, you'll find different ways. Yeah. Having drinks, sending photos (Gail, Firefly).

I think like when we are in office, the events, like, at 4pm, I really enjoy the table tennis. The table tennis - I'd say games (laughing), yeah. I feel good during lockdown 'cause they have some, like, online events always meeting on Zoom so we can do, talk to other people when we want... [WFH] I feel a little bit depressed; I am less connected with people. Like, we are not talking to anyone - work from home every day. So, I feel like I'm always alone (laughing) (Bao, Gecko).

Another significant cultural artefact that has changed in response to hybrid work, is the traditional Friday drinks that used to occur regularly when after work, staff could enjoy a few drinks and some food such as pizza or nibbles with their co-workers. This is because in hybrid work modes, it seems that most people prefer to WFH on Mondays and Fridays, and work in the office on the middle days of the week. I know that my own commute through traffic is worse on Tuesdays, Wednesdays and Thursdays! This could create some continuity in their working week or allow them to extend their weekend a bit by removing a Friday afternoon and Monday morning commute. At Gecko they tried to offset this buy moving their Friday drinks to Thursday late afternoon and progressing into early evening. The Thursday sessions included drinks, both alcoholic and non-alcoholic, a nibbles platter with cheeses and crackers and other finger food, and music provided - either someone playing the guitar, or simply linking a playlist to the sound system. Attendance at Firefly's Friday drinks had also diminished and the People and Culture team sometimes arranged a Thursday get-together for similar reasons to Gecko workers, but overall, this long-held cultural tradition has mostly disappeared from both offices.

Throughout all of my research on humour and fun, workers and managers have always talked to me about food at work. I have even published one academic paper on this topic as it seems quite important to people (Plester, 2014). Therefore, I have noted that food is an important cultural feature enjoyed by workers and that it is also often linked to fun because many events at work feature food (and drink). Both Gecko and Firefly supply coffee, some food, and vending machines full of soft drinks in their office kitchens. For people working at home, company-supplied food and drink is not available, and some workers noted that they missed some of these aspects of office life. At Gecko, Daisy takes responsibility for stocking the fruit bowl and the drinks fridge, organising food for large and small events, and for running the popcorn maker at random times in the office. It is notable that as receptionist, Daisy is one of the few employees that does not regularly work at home. In her words:

> One thing that I find really fun here, is I love our Thursday nibbles, drinks and music …last week we started doing this funny thing at the moment, we'd be like highs and lows of the week so far, like as a joke. And it could be personal, or professional, like just having beers. And, you know what I like, I find that fun and what else do I find fun? I find it fun surprising the team, different things, like we got bagels…, but for me I'm like that's fun for me… So we're having a [company] birthday party, and I've decided to make it a kids theme, like I've got pinatas, lolly [candy] bags… And I know how to make it fun. I love popcorn, so I make popcorn twice a week…Well it's like it's really nice 'cause it's a healthy, it's like a healthy snack. And it makes the office smell warm and then everyone stops, and I make it about two or three times [per week]. And everyone actually stops and goes and gets a bowl, gets a cup, gets up from their desk… companies often forget how much like a little thing goes a long way (Daisy, Gecko).

Nihal also expresses his appreciation for in-office food and drink:

> I love this top kitchen. So, all that, coffee, good food. This is like you know I don't have to worry about carrying my lunch every day or worrying about food or drink or anything like that, so that does help - this is a part of good quality of life so especially the fruits and everything. I've been in places where there was no fruit, no coffee machine, powder coffee - and it was like - I hated that. And especially when you have to go out and buy coffee, it's quite expensive yes (Nihal, Gecko).

Benefits such as office coffee and food are somewhat lost in hybrid work models but both companies have maintained these for the days when staff are in the office and perhaps these are even more appreciated when they are only available on the two or three days when a worker comes into the physical premises.

HAPPINESS IN HYBRID CULTURE

This chapter has explored the idea of cultural changes in fun companies that permit hybrid work with WFH allowed on two or three days of the week. The voices of participants have illustrated the significance and impact that hybrid work is having on their organisational culture especially as both studied companies highly value their fun culture. Fun has changed and become less spontaneous, less event-oriented, less physically interactive. Artefacts of fun such as the ubiquitous table tennis table are being abandoned and new forms of fun are emerging such as zoom chats, online quizzes, shared memes, and post-a-photo competitions. Fun therefore has become less organic in some ways and is more orchestrated (managed) by motivated workers such as People and Culture leaders and culture champions. However, this change in fun and fun cultures does not necessarily have a negative impact on worker happiness. The flexibility of hybrid work reduces commuting time, is family (and pet)-friendly, and demonstrates that individual workers are trusted to work independently. Hybrid work can allow some more focused work as distractions such as water-cooler chats and other social interaction may not permeate the WFH environment. The flexibility of some days co-located in the office and some days working individually at home with technological connection, seems to offer multiple advantages to these workers. Every single participant acclaimed their hybrid work model, clearly stating that they want to continue working in this manner and would find it very difficult to return to fulltime in-office hours. The cultural trade-offs of former fun pursuits and social exchanges are compensated by the flexibility and life-balance offered in their current 'hybrid happiness'.

References

Abril, D. Retrieved September 17, 2024, from https://www.washingtonpost.com/business/2024/09/16/amazon-return-to-office-five-days-week/

Al-Shammari, M. M. (1992). Organisational climate. *Leadership & Organisation Development Journal, 13*(6), 30–32.

Celestine, N. A., & Yeo, G. (2021). Having some fun with it: A theoretical review and typology of activity-based play-at-work. *Journal of Organisational Behavior, 42*(2), 252–268.

Csikszentmihalyi, M., Csikszentmihalyi, M., Abuhamdeh, S., & Nakamura, J. (2014). Flow. *Flow and the foundations of positive psychology: The collected works of Mihaly Csikszentmihalyi.* 227–238.

Ghosh, K., Sinha, S., & Sharma, D. (2023). Virtual fun in a virtual workplace: employee socialization for "work from home". *Benchmarking: An International Journal, 30*(10), 4632–4650.

Freud, S. (1905). *Jokes and their relation to the unconscious.* (A. Richards, Trans. 1991). Penguin.

Hoy, W. K. (1990). Organisational Climate and Culture: A Conceptual Analysis of the School Workplace. *Journal of Educational and Psychological Consultation, 1*(2), 149–168. https://doi.org/10.1207/s1532768xjepc0102_4

Plester, B. A. (2014). Ingesting the organisation: The embodiment of organisational food rituals. *Culture and Organisation, 21*(3), 251–268.

Plester, B. A. (2016). *The complexity of workplace humour: Laughter, jokers and the dark side*. Springer.

Plester, B., Cooper-Thomas, H., & Winquist, J. (2015). The fun paradox. *Employee Relations, 37*(3), 380–398.

Plester, B., & Hutchison, A. (2016). Fun times: The relationship between fun and workplace engagement. *Employee Relations, 38*(3), 332–350.

Schein, E. H. (1985, 2004). *Organisational culture and leadership*. Jossey Bass.

Schneider, B., Ehrhart, M. G., & Macey, W. H. (2011). Perspectives on organisational climate and culture. In S. Zedeck (Ed.), *APA handbook of industrial and organisational psychology, Vol. 1. Building and developing the organisation* (pp. 373–414). American Psychological Association. https://doi.org/10.1037/12169-012.

Stanko, T. L., Dahm, P. C., Lahneman, B., & Richter, J. (2022). Navigating an Identity Playground: Using sociomateriality to build a theory of identity play. *Organisation Studies, 43*, 81–103.

Trice, H. M., & Beyer, J. M. (1993). *The cultures of work organisations*. Prentice-Hall, Inc.

CHAPTER 4

Psychological Safety in Hybrid Fun

SAFE VERSUS UNSAFE FUN

Throughout my research I became aware that people sometimes talked about fun and humour as workplace activities that could be 'risky'. This intrigued me and I tried to explore and develop this notion of risk within fun through questioning and analysing my data to see if there was evidence that risk was inherently involved in workplace fun and humour. Intuitively I sensed that fun could be risky as in some of my early workplace research I had seen instances of fun and humour played out and some of these appeared borderline, potentially offensive, upsetting, and even physically unsafe. Therefore, I approached my hybrid work research with this concept of risk percolating, and I formulated some questions to explore this angle of fun and humour. My specific questions asked participants whether they felt physically safe and also whether they felt psychologically safe when participating in fun at work, including both in-person and online fun.

As I researched, I found little to no evidence of physical risk in my studied workplaces because organisations are very careful to comply with health and safety regulations imposed and developed by government, industry moderators, and unions. What became strikingly apparent was that risk in humour and fun interactions was perceived in relation to emotional aspects of work pertaining to self-image, dignity, and career aspirations. Through deep data analysis, the concept of *psychological safety* emerged as important to the workers in my study. Therefore, I further unpacked this concept linking it to hybrid work and in particular exploring its relationship with fun, humour, and overall wellbeing. I was keen to explore how psychological safety might impact upon social aspects of workplace relations and to evaluate how people behave when working between the office and remote work. It emerged that for fun and humour to flourish at work, people need to feel safe enough to engage in light-hearted activities and to express themselves through humour and laughter. Psychological safety is underpinned (or not) by the overall workplace climate which needs to be supportive for people to feel safe and subsequently enjoy fun and humour at work.

Careful analysis of what interview participants described, plus observations of their behaviour in the office and online, has indicated a circular relationship between fun and psychological safety. This means that while workers need to feel safe to enjoy fun at work, at the same time when leaders instigate fun or humour, they can make people feel safer by demonstrating that fun and humour are acceptable and encouraged. Thus, the relationship between fun and safety is one where feeling safe allows fun to flourish and simultaneously, having fun can create a feeling of safety. However, there are conditions to such a relationship and fun that fails, or humour that crosses a line can create feelings of unsafety, and discomfort. Like all relationships, its complicated!

My most recent research with Dr. Rhiannon Lloyd, elicited several interesting themes linked to the relationship between psychological safety and fun in hybrid work. In this chapter I use these three themes to demonstrate the relationship between fun, safety, and leadership at work. I would like to acknowledge that the themes were developed within an academic paper with Rhiannon (Plester & Lloyd, 2023) and these are:

1. Unsafe fun
2. Safety to be yourself
3. Leadership influence.

The themes offer some nuanced insights into understanding individual worker preferences, leadership, and psychological climates that permit and encourage workers to enjoy fun. They also suggest that a 'no-strings, opt-out' clause is a useful option for those who prefer not to participate in fun activities. Before exploring the themes, it is important to discuss the concept of psychological safety and some of the theory underpinning this construct.

PSYCHOLOGICAL SAFETY

The concept of psychological safety (psych safety) has gained substantial attention in management studies over the last decade. The term conceptualises workers' perceptions of their workplace environment in regard to the freedom to express ideas and thoughts without having to fear adverse consequences such as humiliation, exclusion, or punishment (Edmondson, 1999). More recent notions of psychological safety understand it as a shared team or organisational belief whereby workers can safely ask for help, take risks, speak up, express their ideas, disagreement, or concerns without fear of negative reprisal involving embarrassment, disadvantages, or punishment (Frazier et al, 2017). Psychological safety is intrinsically linked to climates of workplace safety, trust, and collegiality which suggests some strong overlap with conceptions of organisational fun (Edmondson & Lei, 2014). There are many obvious benefits of psych safety including information sharing, creativity, innovation, idea generation, stronger individual and team performance, and risk-taking. (Edmondson & Lei, 2014; Edmondson & Roloff, 2008; Edmondson & Mogelof, 2006; Newman et al., 2017). Psychological safety has also been linked to positive individual outcomes such as job satisfaction, engagement, and commitment (Frazier et al.,'s 2017). Angel's comments below illustrate the notion of psychological safety that she experiences in her workplace and how this fosters openness and the ability to try things:

> Here, the trust is high. The processes are followed, that everybody gets fair and equitable assessment of their work. So, I feel safe in my actual job, I feel safe in that, if I found in my job that I kind of wanted to change it was, like, actually, this is in my long-term future goals… I feel safe that I can be honest about the things I want to change about being here. And, someone will say, sure, and I think they're trying really, from what I observe of the People and Culture team. They try really hard, like, people feel safe enough to tell us if you want to look for another job. And what can we do to keep you here, and if we can't keep you here, we'll send you on your way happily. I think for people here who are super young they haven't been in workplaces where, you know, there may be, hopefully there are not, but there may be shocks in their future if they leave and go

to big organisations. Where this level of safety is not a given....at least I'm in a place where I feel safe enough to do the scary things (Angel, Gecko).

Psychological safety is a shared workplace belief that is firmly influenced by the work environment (Newman et al., 2017). Some early research closely examined psychological climates exploring the shared perceptions and attitudes of employees that incorporated organisational values, norms, and generally considered the overall work atmosphere (Brown & Leigh, 1996). A Psychological Safety Climate (PSC) considers the extent to which employees identify their work environment as psychologically and socially, supportive and safe (Bond et al., 2010). An organisation that is ethical, trusts its workers, prioritises employees' well-being, fosters a healthy work environment, and is seen to have a positive work culture is likely to have a PSC (Dollard et al., 2017). Such positive PSC's are credited with being more adaptable, innovative, better at organisational learning and knowledge exchange, more open, and resilient (Carmeli, 2007; Carmeli & Gittell, 2009; Edmondson & Lei, 2014).

Fun Climate

Organisational climate and culture are important underpinning factors in both psychological safety and fun. Fun at work is embedded in organisational culture which determines what fun can occur, what activities are promoted and encouraged, and what types of fun prevail or are discouraged (Plester, 2009). Organisational culture and climate are key determinants of the fun experience in a workplace. Many organisations are keen to promote themselves as having a fun culture (Karl & Peluchette, 2006; Plester, 2009) and enthusiastic endorsement and promotion of processing a fun culture became popular in the nineteen eighties and nineties and still prevails in many modern workplaces. A fun culture is perceived as a relaxed and supportive environment that facilitates, encourages, and supports a variety of pleasurable formal and informal fun activities (Ford et al., 2003). Work environments may even be planned and designed to promote managerially sanctioned forms of fun (Bolton & Houlihan, 2009). For example, bright colours and play equipment may permeate some offices with the now-classic example offered by the Google campus (or Googleplex), famous for funky spaces and structures designed to foster fun and creativity.

The work environment is still perceived as a social place where colleagues are co-located, and the office may include spaces for socialisation that enhance fun through co-worker interaction and special events. Workplaces that recognise and allow space for socialising also promote casual, spontaneous, organic fun where workers and managers mingle and create their own fun through chat, banter, laughter, food, eating and drinking, and even light-hearted horseplay and games (Plester et al., 2015; Tews et al., 2014). Organic fun occurs naturally when the work climate is conducive to fun, and workplaces that make fun part of their organisational identity signal to employees that management supports and encourages fun and this usually creates a safe space for expressions of fun.

Organisational leadership is an important element in order to develop psychologically safe cultures that encourage and value diverse perspectives, collaboration and supports risk-taking (Edmondson & Lei, 2014). To maintain a psychologically safe climate, leaders must prioritise employee well-being and a positive organisational culture featuring trust, transparency, and accountability (Law et al., 2011). Without leadership endorsement, employees are not as likely to participate in pro-social work behaviours such as collaboration and fun (Bienefeld & Grote, 2014). Leadership that clearly models and encourages positive, fun interactions fosters a PSC that is seen as less risky, which creates a higher likelihood of workers participating fully in fun activities.

Risky Fun

Risk is related to both psychological safety and fun and this was evident when research participants discussed their experiences of hybrid work and fun when working. It seems that risk has increased when working in a hybrid mode due to uncertainties about new norms and expectations when having fun at work and these workers and managers question what is (or isn't) appropriate in their new work mode as they evaluate the new risks of having fun:

> Because it's almost like there's a judgement element of fun. It's like I want to join in. But will I be accepted and will it be, okay? I think it is - like sometimes - I think it's risky. (Hamish, Firefly).

The trouble is the world's changing, too. And I think if we are not careful, we will knock the playfulness out of anything that we do. Because everything becomes a taboo that we're not allowed to do or talk about and I think we are on the cusp of, if we're not careful, you know, that we are going to become too frightened to say anything. (Andy, Firefly).

Risky fun may encompass a wide range of activities and interactions ranging from inappropriate humor to off-task behaviour, and some physical activities that confer psychological risk (such as dress up days as discussed in earlier chapters). From interviews with workers and managers, and from my observations, it seems that organic fun may be more susceptible to unexpected risk because organic fun is usually unauthorised, unmanaged, and spontaneous. Workplace fun varies greatly between different work contexts dependent on diverse factors such as formality, industry, occupation and team dynamics (Plester, 2016). As we can see in the extracts above, people are now also struggling to judge the appropriateness of workplace fun within hybrid work as they work out what fun is now acceptable both online and in-person. Hamish describes fun as 'risky' and Andy mentions 'taboos' and being 'frightened' to have fun at work, suggesting that fun may disappear. It seems that in moving to hybrid work workers are unsure of how fun should be enacted now and that it feels risky as they work out the new norms and protocols.

There is an extra element to riskiness in fun that can occur in forced (managed) fun. The notion of forced fun where workers feel compelled to join fun activities even if they do not enjoy them, may seem harmless, innocuous, and positive, but earlier research shows that such contrived creation of fun can cause distress, cynicism, loss of dignity and a feeling of being patronised by management (Fleming, 2005; Plester et al., 2015). Jasper (below) discusses how he felt when he had to join a simulated catwalk fun event where staff were asked to model their Covid outfits—the assumption being that people wore business attire on their top half as this was visible in online video calls, while wearing their pyjamas or similar on the invisible lower half of their body for comfort and ease.

> I mean, like, there is space to have fun. Yeah. However you want. There's a lot of what I'd call 'forced fun'. Sometimes they make you do things in the name of fun that I don't find fun. Yeah, I feel like that's a pretty standard workplace. thing, right... maybe a couple of months ago, there was this catwalk - scenario thing, I don't know if people were dressed up or not, just, I wanted no part of it. But it was all just happening, like right

down here. And we were being pressured to take part in the name of fun. And not remotely. Really punishing. Yeah. And you were notable if you avoided it. I put a minimal effort. Yeah. That's but you know, I can see it being a little more difficult for somebody who is not really interested in that particular sort of thing. But I can see if that is a new person's idea of not fun, then they might struggle. They might have struggled in that. What one person finds fun there's often not what everybody likes - I would call it 'horrors'. Like I didn't see the point. It wasn't fun, and there wasn't a benefit. There wasn't a benefit… It's always forced. It's very like - performative. Like - 'look, everybody - look how fun we are. Look how much fun we're having'…But just, that particular incident was really like, yeah, they made everybody get up and do this catwalk in front of everybody. And I can very much see that not being everybody's idea of fun - that they struggle with (Jasper, Firefly).[1]

Jasper's words convey a strongly emotive dislike for this event which he gamely participated in due to the expectations of his managers and co-workers. He keenly observes that it is 'notable if you avoided it' suggesting he felt forced to participate. It seems he felt confronted and unsafe during this activity as he calls it 'horrors', 'performative', and 'pointless', as he notes the 'struggle' for himself and others. So, although it is tempting to assume that managerially endorsed fun is enjoyable for everyone, power dynamics in the workplace may constrain frontline workers such as Jasper from complaining or opting out as they may perceive a threat to their career progression, workplace relationships, or work conditions. A second risk of non-participation is in being seen as humourless, fun-less, or worst of all in an organisation, as 'not—a—team—player'. Jasper found himself in a no-win situation and opted for minimal participation even while feeling extreme emotional discomfort. He was strongly influenced by workplace dynamics such as team norms, perceptions of belongingness, and organisational engagement. I'm not claiming that fun in hybrid work is always risky. Rather, I am suggesting that it is definitely worth questioning what types of workplace fun are experienced as 'unfun' by some people when it makes them feel exposed, undignified, and unsafe—like Jasper. Post-research, I worked with the organisation from where this example arose and we agreed that managed

---

[1] This chapter contains previously published excerpts from the Open Access publication: Frontiers of Psychology Happiness Is 'Being Yourself': Psychological Safety and Fun in Hybrid Work. https://www.mdpi.com/2076-3387/13/10/218

fun events need to have an opt-out clause where no questions are asked or no pressure is applied should someone decline to participate. This might help somewhat in situations like Jasper's but it still likely that he would feel a normative pressure to perform as part of the team he belongs to, implying that types of fun may need to be assessed or even anonymous polls circulated when developing fun events. Happily, in the Firefly company when I discussed this issue (keeping Jasper anonymous) they decided that workers could, and should, feel safe enough to express such discomfort, and senior managers confirmed that diverse sensitivities would be considered for future events. I note here that Jasper was not the only person that felt affronted by some workplace fun events, but he was perhaps the most eloquent in his dismay.

Fun and humour are complex, and exchanges can quickly sour if people are subjected to workplace humour or fun that makes them uncomfortable. Whereas above, the participants describe the ways managed fun undermines psychological safety, the quotes below specifically discuss humour in social interactions with colleagues. They highlight the delicate balance required for psych safety where people should be enabled to be themselves at work and take some risks (in humour and fun), but that such risks can also undermine psych safety. Jack notes that he sometimes feels upset about humour that targets him (if he's having a 'quiet day') while Naomi highlights a colleague with a dark sense of humour that she struggles with because it opposes her own 'light', 'childlike', 'nice', humour.

> I make jokes. I always try and be real careful not to make personal jokes. 'Cause, I like making jokes, you kind of learn, like, what kind of jokes are okay. And I know what kind of jokes aren't okay and I don't say them. And so, I'll definitely push the boundaries but in a, like, a very thought-out controlled way. But people don't always pick up on that, and so because people see me as, like, you like making jokes they'll make personal jokes at me. In a way to kind of do what I do, and I, sort of, get, like, I'm kind of sensitive, I'll be, like, that's, like, that's just, like, a personal dig guys - as a joke, like, that's not what I'm doing… And so, it tends to just be, like, people go, you're the joke guy I can make fun of you, and you can take it. Or, like, you're a tall white dude, like, I can make jokes about you, that's fine. And sometimes it does kind of get to the point where I'm, like that's just not funny. But it rarely happens and it's not so much at work, but when it does, I'll kind of just shrug it off 'cause it's not that big of a

deal. But, when I'm having a quiet day, it does kind of upset me a little bit more (Jack, Gecko).

Max - has you know that sense of humor? Like, it's a bit more of a dark kind of sense of humor. You know, it's like kind of sarcastic you know, that kind of sarcastic calling people down - that kind of way. So - targeted at someone - maybe a little bit more targeted. So, some people in the office love that. I know a lot of people do love that kind of humor, but I struggle. I struggle with it. I'm quiet. I have a light, very light, childlike kind of nice humor (Naomi, Firefly).

Risk-taking is a desirable aspect of psychologically safe organisation and considered to be highly beneficial for innovative, creative workplaces (Edmondson & Mogelof, 2008) and risk-taking is inherently a part of sharing humour and fun with others, especially work colleagues. Psychological safety involves interpersonal risk (Baer & Frese, 2003) when workers share ideas, speak up, question processes without fearing negative consequences such as criticism and ridicule and it as equally part of the process of sharing fun and humour at work. Workers who feel unsafe are unlikely to create, promote, or even participate in humour and fun. Although feeling psychologically safe can potentially encourage more fun at work, the inverse relationship occurs when fun undermines psych safety as seen in the example with Jasper who experienced pressure to perform in his workplace fun event resulting in personal stress, discomfort, and embarrassment. A different event may have been enjoyable for him, and this highlights the complexity of workplace fun that is experienced in alternative ways due to individual differences and preferences. A final contextual point is that Jasper and colleagues had worked at home for long periods of time during lockdowns and this event was one of the first organised in the office space upon their return. After being physically isolated for some time it may have been too confronting to be asked to strut down a catwalk modelling a funny outfit, especially for those with a more introverted nature. Again, this highlights the individual nature of some fun while also suggesting that that hybrid work is changing peoples' acceptance of what is and is not fun and many workers may now prefer online fun to performative in-person fun.

As noted earlier, the ability to opt out of fun might help people who feel confronted or uncomfortable with some forms of fun. Opting out is probably easier to achieve in online fun, for example simply not logging on to the quiz, or not commenting on the latest thread of quips and quotes. However, opting out in-person can be tricky to achieve as normative pressures can result in forced fun that may not be easily avoided—as happened to Jasper. Many of my interviewees clearly identified their personality as 'introverted' and therefore they were not keen to actively participate in fun that was loud, performative, or that made them highly visible. Irene is one such person and her she discusses her positioning in workplace fun:

> My personality is that I like to stand back in the dark and watch people have fun. So like, I don't - yeah - I don't really join in, or you know - self-express too much. But when I see people having fun I feel happy inside. Oh, so yeah, I stay back, and I watch people have fun… They don't force you. But they invite you… I feel like our whole team as a whole is very, very cheerful and happy. Like, the reason why I like to go to work every day. You know, it's like informal, but like still professional. They overwork themselves. I have to say they work very hard. But I'm happy that they have a little bit of fun. they work hard and play hard… Everyone says they feel safe, safe to be themselves, safe to join the fun or safe to take a step back (Irene, Firefly).

Note that Irene is happy for her colleagues to have fun—she even feels happy seeing their fun, but she personally likes to 'stay back' and 'watch'. She feels invited into fun rather than forced to join in and emphasises that she feels safe to either join or as is her obvious preference, opt out. In contrast Naomi (below) who enjoys workplace fun, also avoids it sometimes as it can be 'too much'. Having the choice to disengage from fun is an important factor that forms part of workers' psychological safety.

> I almost feel like there's a bit too much of it [fun] at the moment and workloads are quite high and I've kind of been actively avoiding it… so that was a choice, all those things happening in that week, that was just a choice if you wanted to be in it fine. If you're busy - just get on with things (Naomi, Firefly).

If opting out is respected and normalised, then workers will feel psychologically safe around fun activities and like Irene, may even enjoy the enjoyment of their colleagues, whether or not they get involved.

JUST BE YOURSELF!

This section includes more of the positive aspects of the relationship between workplace fun and psych safety. When asking participants about fun many of them talked about the ability to 'be yourself' in the workplace. They equated the freedom of 'being yourself' with psych safety and saw it as an important element if they are to enjoy fun at work. Therefore, I explored the interrelationship of psychological safety and 'being yourself' as it seemed integral to the experience of fun at work for the people I studied. Expressing personal and authentic aspects of the self was linked to being 'silly' and 'playful' when having fun, as conveyed by Naomi:

> I just feel like I can be my true self at work and hopefully allow others to be their true selves... it's quite comfortable, isn't it? If you can be your true self at work?... you can express yourself through fun and your play at work... it's amazing. I can be silly and playful, which is my true kind of nature. (Naomi, Firefly).

Daniel further explains how being yourself relates to being able to joke and even swear without censure. It is notable that he also points out that this is okay as long as people are not offended but does not articulate how he determines offence and what might happen if someone is offended. Jack talks about 'dropping his guard' which he sees as part of feeling safe enough to enjoy events and his colleagues. Comments like these are peppered throughout my interview transcripts and it seems that safety is a prerequisite to being your true self which in turn fosters fun and enjoyment as discussed here:

> And everybody can just be themselves and, and crack jokes and people swear a lot as well. Yeah, it's not, it's not, you know, frowned upon. As long as you're not, you know, offending anyone directly. and I feel like people who swear a lot are somewhat more trustworthy as well because they just, you know, they show their emotions, they're not hiding it, you know (Daniel, Gecko).

> [We have] more classic fun which is, like, you know, social events and hanging out with people at lunch. Which generally is, you know, as frequent as I could ever want it, and that's always a lot of fun. Like, the people at Gecko I get along with very well. A lot of them I, sort of, call them friends and, yeah, we generally have a good time and are able

to, sort of, put the guard down a little bit and just kind of enjoy being human which is nice (Jack, Gecko).

Andy, a health and well-being manager in the People and Culture team associates workplace fun with happiness and links these concepts to trust in his workmates. As the focus of his job is ensuring health and well-being for colleagues, he raised the idea of psych safety himself. His focus on workplace happiness is optimistic, positive, and obvious here:

> Because happiness for me is that you have fun while you're at work, you trust the people you work with. But I can say that, you know, that if we if we stick to these principles of psychological safety, you know, and psychosocial risk assessments, and just general, nice operating standards, then, I think by-product of that is the bigger the happier workforce (Andy, Firefly).

The overarching argument in this section and key takeaway point is that fostering an environment where workers feel safe allows them to authentically reveal more of themselves which engenders a workplace climate that is more conducive to fun. Such an environment may foster more organic and spontaneous types of fun that often occur in workplaces with fun cultures. This may make workers feel happier and encourage greater participation in events, activities, and interactions online and in person, and this is important in blended workplace models where people are working in both contexts.

Leading Fun

Leaders have a significant impact on workplace psych safety and also on the climate that supports or constrains workplace fun. Some leaders use humour effectively and making a self-deprecating joke is viewed as open and supportive which can make subordinate workers feel increased psych safety. Leaders' humour can also make failure seem less threatening while fostering inclusion and safety (Almeida & Josten, 2021). Research participants included many leaders such as managers, CEOs, company founders, and team leaders. I usually manage to spend time with the People and Culture teams (or HR department if using this terminology) and it is always useful to compare leaders' answers to interview questions with that of subordinate workers. Analysis involves identifying cohesive points of alignment while also exploring key differences. For example, in some of my earlier research in a law firm, HR leaders and the CEO firmly declared that they were a 'fun company' while junior lawyers and other subordinate workers strongly (and crossly) disagreed saying that this was impossible due to expectations and pressures of their industry. In my most recent project the senior leaders were all navigating workplace changes experienced through the implementation and increase in hybrid work. As my focus was fun and how this may have changed or be in the process of changing, I was able to ask leaders and subordinates specific questions about how fun was being experienced in hybrid work mode, and how they were coping with the social aspects of hybrid work.

Below, Gecko company founder Dev talks about psych safety and trust as important to fun within work teams. In contrast well-being manager, Andy, points out that some joking must be regulated to protect workers from offence and harm. It seems that Andy feels a managerial responsibility for this regulation and some 'policing' of fun, thereby ensuring psych safety by limiting fun and /or humour that might be contentious.

> We've lost that opportunity for pulling teams together, and seeing teams grow together. And building that sense of sort of psychological trust in a team that says, we're allowed to have fun, we're allowed to have a crack, break, because we're a team. And we can do we can say things and do things that are only a good, strong, safe team can do. And I think it's a shame that we've, where we've, I think we want it. But it's almost like we're having to start again (Dev, Founder, Gecko).

> So, there's a few jokes that have been made, which are potentially not PC - we need to be PC in the workplace, to accept all different cultures, people's beliefs and everything as well. So, if we step over the line, there's one or two people, which might be really offended by that. Yeah. And then we just kind of pull them aside, say 'hey, look, just letting you know the management team's onto it.' You might have a quiet word... So, it's like, I think one example of someone come through on WhatsApp group for work. A comment was made. And I just said, 'probably that's not okay, I think.' No - no - I talked to them individually. Yeah. And then it was almost like, 'maybe remove the comment.' I think that's not something you really want recorded in a place and maybe we need a policy to proactively send an apology rather than wait for that... So, if you're on the management team - it's kind of it's part of your responsibility to make sure people are appropriate. I think even from a management lens, we try

not to be the police even though people do say it's like the police sometimes... We're not policing people. We're policing respect... If people do something a little bit cheeky, a little bit fun, a little bit playful, like, don't pull it up. But if it's that starts to affect someone else, that's when you step in (Andy, Firefly).

Alternatively, Joseph a project manager talks about people who create fun but at the same time notes the 'permissibility' to champion fun. This implies that although fun is allowed, there are still leadership influences overseeing their workplace fun. Odette a junior employee talks about safety and her nervousness when interacting with the CEO on her first day. However, he made her feel safe by his joking and laughing with her which fostered a feeling of psych safety for her that has continued as she has become more socialised into her workplace.

> So, like, so we ended up having these, like, sort of informal, you know, like culture champions? I mean, we don't - yeah - so they're informal. That's good. Yeah. I mean, I mean, like, people have permissibility to, to do that. And so so you really see like people who sort of step up... Those people, either the culture champions or the Jokers the ones who were kind of quite keen on making it all happen (Joseph, Firefly).

> I don't think I'd stay in a job if I didn't feel safe, or I'd like to think I wouldn't anyway. I think it was day one and I was sitting, like, my first ever role day one intern and I was sitting opposite the CEO. And I was scared, like, I was scared, I was nervous on my first ever day 'cause I'd heard what CEOs were meant to be. But within five minutes, he was like, laughing and joking around ... he always asks me to tell him when someone new is starting so he can go over and, like, personally introduce himself which is nice. And kind of make sure that they know who he is and that they can go to him, as well... when I was interning here, like, I felt completely safe, as well (Odette, Gecko).

These reflective comments confirm the relationship between psych safety and fun while also depicting some significant implications for leaders. If a senior leader can make successful jokes and model some lighthearted fun this can create psych safety in junior workers and show that workplace fun is acceptable and encouraged. Dev reinforces this through noting that when people feel safe in their work teams, they can have fun together. The leaders in this section accept responsibility for fun by reinforcing safety through some constraints while also encouraging lighthearted forms of fun at work. This takes different forms ranging from modelling fun themselves, to speaking to subordinates that may have gone too far and crossed the line into fun that has the potential to offend or harm. Again, I note the complexity of these social dynamics and suggest that this is made even more complex by having responsibility for both in-person (office) fun, alongside online fun. Leaders must now consider streamed content including comments in channels such as WhatsApp, or online platforms such as Slack and chat streams on online platforms such as Zoom and other similar workplace platforms.

A Complex Relationship

This chapter questions how experiences of psychological safety and workplace fun overlap in hybrid work and explores implications for workplace relations. I have presented three thematic sections to illustrate the significance of new fun experiences in relation to psych safety for both leaders and subordinate workers in hybrid work. The themes show how psych safety and fun at work are connected in complex ways. In this summative section I bring these dynamics together to suggest workplace and managerial implications for interested readers, workers, leaders, and HR or People and Culture teams.

Managed fun was openly discussed by many participants, and it is a type of packaged fun, that may be organised and promoted by different workplace leaders. The theme exploring the idea of risk in workplace fun depicts some of the challenges in the relationship between psych safety and fun. Feeling compelled to join workplace fun can feel risky if it is not an activity perceived as fun by some people and participating unwillingly can make workers feel uncomfortable and unsafe. Workers must weigh up the risks of participating reluctantly and anxiously versus not participating at all with the possibility of being judged for this. This indecision fosters anxiety that can be detrimental to their well-being, ironically within experiences ostensibly created to foster happiness and good feelings. I shared a specific example where one worker felt threatened by joining a fun event and could not see a safe way to opt out, therefore he simply endured and participated in the most minimal way possible. A fun event that feels forced may negatively impact the workplace climate for some workers (Bond et al., 2010) and result in negative emotions and anxiety. Therefore, while it is important to encourage fun at work that might have a range of benefits for some workers, fun also provokes mixed reactions among individual workers.

I argue that the relationship between psych safety and fun is circular in that workers need to feel safe in order to enjoy and participate in fun, through feeling that it is acceptable and appropriate. At the same time, some fun and joking especially when modelled by workplace leaders can actually make a workplace feel safer and can make some workers feel more comfortable. It is notable that getting involved in workplace fun can reveal aspects of the self and this can be both beneficial and positive or can be experienced as problematic and confronting to some people. While many workers can enjoy having fun, maybe being a bit silly, they also need to have the option to withdraw when work needs to take precedence or they simply don't feel like getting involved. Therefore, my suggested safety feature of an opt out clause is an important consideration for several reasons, including personal feelings and work priorities. Freedom is important in fun (Michel et al., 2019; Tews et al., 2014) and is a key component in the interrelationship between fun and psych safety.

With the move to more hybrid work, fun may need to be championed and modelled by leaders. Seeing fun displayed by senior leaders can create psych safety for junior workers and in these newer forms of work may need to be displayed in-person and online so that both environments are seen as safe. At the same time there seems to be a need for senior leaders to limit and constrain some fun or humour types ensure psych safety and wellbeing as they reinforce company values and constructive ethical cultures. When fun and humour cross the line and violate organisational or societal norms, both become highly risky activities (see Plester, 2009, 2016).

Workplace leaders need to understand the nuance and complexity of fun in order to support psych safety and develop a PSC. This involves respecting individual workers' boundaries and personality characteristics such as introversion. Opting out should not be judged as a lack of team engagement but as a sign that a specific event or interaction is not enjoyable for a worker, or that in that particular moment they do not feel like joining the fun. Jollying workers into participating may have poor results that are not always apparent. Organisational leaders play an important role in fostering fun while also allowing judgement-free non-participation. Simultaneously they need to maintain boundaries to fun and humour in order to safeguard everyone in the workplace. This requires a nuanced understanding of fun, and awareness of what is occurring both in the office and in online interactions.

My prior research has shown that workers prefer organic forms of fun that occur naturally and spontaneously within a safe work environment. However, this type of fun has an unmanaged quality and it can be risky, albeit a mostly positive risk. The rules of organic fun are fluid and ambiguous and the new conditions of hybrid work increase the complexity and risk for managers and workers as organisations strive to stay psychologically safe. Leaders have a tricky task as they establish and maintain conditions where workers can be authentically themselves at work. This mean that those that want to be silly, playful, and light-hearted can do so while others can simply maintain their workflow uninterrupted. Working online creates greater challenges for spontaneous organic fun, but creative workers are finding ever-increasing ways to preserve their spirit of fun across online platforms through using visual technological tools such as emojis, gifs, and memes. Hybrid work may actually help promote favourable conditions as someone opting out of an online game or quiz is not as highly visible as an unsmiling non-participating worker in office fun activities. I suggest that new practices of fun are emerging organically, and much hybrid fun is trial and error for each individual and company. For the most part, it seems that organisations are balancing this quite well with a few slip ups that offer learning scenarios for future endeavours. Organisational leaders can encourage some experimentation and People and Culture teams may do well to fully debrief after fun activities garnering feelings and reactions to inform future events.

I have explored the complex, circular relationship between psych safety and workplace fun emphasising the essential elements of risk, authenticity (be yourself), and leadership required to successfully promote and encourage fun in hybrid work. Not all fun is good fun, and a nuanced, sensitive understanding of this concept is important. Additionally, recognising elements that establish psych safety must be balanced against individual preferences and requirements of fun at work. Hybrid work creates significant interpersonal ambiguity in fun interactions because these are now a blend of online and in-person events that can be difficult to navigate. Workplace well-being and happiness is important to workers and managers and fostering an inclusive environment for fun can promote morale and a positive culture. A psychologically safe workplace climate allows authentic self-expression, creativity, and some spontaneous fun interactions, can contribute to a workplace where fun occurs naturally, and enhances happiness online and in the office.

References

Almeida, T., & Josten, C. (2021). Not a joke: leveraging humor at work increases performance, individual happiness, and psychological safety. *LSE Business Review* (28 Apr. p.3). http://eprints.lse.ac.uk/110560/1/businessreview_2021_04_28_not_a_joke_leveraging_humor_at_work.pdf

Baer, M., & Frese, M. (2003). Innovation is not enough: Climates for initiative and psychological safety, process innovations, and firm performance. *Journal of Organisational Behaviour: THe International Journal of Industrial, Occupational and Organisational Psychology and Behaviour, 24*(1), 45–68.

Bienefeld, N., & Grote, G. (2014). Speaking up in ad hoc multiteam systems: Individual-level effects of psychological safety, status, and leadership within and across teams. *European Journal of Work and Organisational Psychology, 23*(6), 930–945.

Bolton, S. C., & Houlihan, M. (2009). Are we having fun yet? A consideration of workplace fun and engagement. *Employee Relations, 31*(6), 556–568.

Bond, S. A., Tuckey, M. R., & Dollard, M. F. (2010). Psychosocial safety climate, workplace bullying, and symptoms of posttraumatic stress. *Organisation Development Journal, 28*(1), 37.

Brown, S. P., & Leigh, T. W. (1996). A new look at psychological climate and its relationship to job involvement, effort, and performance. *Journal of Applied Psychology, 81*(4), 358.

Carmeli, A. (2007). Social capital, psychological safety and learning behaviours from failure in organisations. *Long Range Planning, 40*(1), 30–44.

Carmeli, A., & Gittell, J. H. (2009). High-quality relationships, psychological safety, and learning from failures in work organisation. *Journal of Organisational Behaviour: THe International Journal of Industrial, Occupational and Organisational Psychology and Behaviour, 30*(6), 709–729.

Dollard, M. F., Dormann, C., Tuckey, M. R., & Escartín, J. (2017). Psychosocial safety climate (PSC) and enacted PSC for workplace bullying and psychological health problem reduction. *European Journal of Work and Organisational Psychology, 26*(6), 844–857.

Edmondson, A. (1999). Psychological safety and learning behaviour in work Teams. *Administrative Science Quarterly, 44*(2), 350–383.

Edmondson, A. C., & Lei, Z. (2014). Psychological safety: The history, renaissance, and future of an interpersonal construct. *Annual Review Organisational Psychology & Organisational Behavior, 1*(1), 23–43.

Edmondson, A. C., & Mogelof, J. P. (2006). Explaining psychological safety in innovation teams: Organisational culture, team dynamics, or personality. In Leigh L. Thompson & Hoon-Seok Choi (Eds), *Creativity and Innovation in Organisational Teams*: 109–136.

Edmondson, A. C., & Roloff, K. S. (2008). Overcoming barriers to collaboration: Psychological safety and learning in diverse teams. In E. Salas, G. F.

Goodwin, & C. S. Burke (Eds.), *Team Effectiveness in Complex Organisation* (pp. 217–242). Routledge.

Fleming, P. (2005). Worker's playtime? Boundaries and cynicism in a 'Culture of fun' program. *The Journal of Applied Behavioral Science, 41*(3), 285–303.

Ford, R. C., McLaughlin, F. S., & Newstrom, J. W. (2003). Questions and answers about fun at work. *Human Resource Planning, 26*(4), 18–33.

Frazier, M. L., Fainshmidt, S., Klinger, R. L., Pezeshkan, A., & Vracheva, V. (2017). Psychological safety: A meta-analytic review and extension. *Personnel Psychology, 70*(1), 113–165.

Karl, K., & Peluchette, J. (2006). How does workplace fun impact employee perceptions of customer service quality? *Journal of Leadership and Organisational Studies, 13*(2), 2–13.

Law, R., Dollard, M. F., Tuckey, M. R., & Dormann, C. (2011). Psychosocial safety climate as a lead indicator of workplace bullying and harassment, job resources, psychological health and employee engagement. *Accident Analysis & Prevention, 43*(5), 1782–1793.

Michel, J. W., Tews, M. J., & Allen, D. G. (2019). Fun in the workplace: A review and expanded theoretical perspective. *Human Resource Management Review, 29*(1), 98–110.

Newman, A., Donohue, R., & Eva, N. (2017). Psychological safety: A systematic review of the literature. *Human Resource Management Review, 27*(3), 521–535.

Plester, B. (2009). Crossing the line: Boundaries of workplace humour and fun. *Employee Relations, 31*(6), 584–599.

Plester, B. A. (2016). *The Complexity of Workplace Humour: Laughter, Jokers and the Dark Side*. Springer.

Plester, B., Cooper-Thomas, H., & Winquist, J. (2015). The fun paradox. *Employee Relations, 37*(3), 380–398.

Plester, B. A., & Lloyd, R. (2023). Happiness is 'being yourself': Psychological safety and fun in hybrid work. *Administrative Sciences, 13*(10), 218.

Tews, M. J., Michel, J. W., & Allen, D. G. (2014). Fun and friends: The impact of workplace fun and constituent attachment on turnover in a hospitality context. *Human Relations, 67*, 923–946.

CHAPTER 5

The Emotional Landscape of Hybrid Work

EMOTIONS

Emotions are one of the important, unique qualities that give us our humanity. They are adaptive responses that increase survival and coordinate other systems such as perception, inference, motivation, learning behaviours, and physical responses. Emotions result from experiences and events, or from interpretations of factors in our immediate surroundings. They usually refer to discreet, intense but short-lived experiences that may constitute our instinctive or gut reactions. Emotions are powerful motivators and may be the starting point for responsive actions such as 'fight or flight' when fear is experienced. They are controllable to a degree but less so for very extreme emotions such as those caused by grief (Frijda, 1986; Cooper & Cartwright, 2001). People generally attempt to limit exposure to unpleasant emotions (such as sadness and fear) and increase exposure to pleasant emotions (such as happiness) experienced in desirable situations.

Based on research by psychologist Paul Ekman examining facial expressions, it is somewhat accepted by evolutionary theorists that there are six basic emotions, and these are: happiness, sadness, disgust, anger, fear, and surprise. It is believed that all other emotions result from blends of these primary emotions. Contrastingly, Discrete Emotion Theory argues for 12 emotions, Aristotle identified eight, and Charles Darwin listed 34 different emotions! More recently, researchers from the University of

California, Berkeley identified 27 categories of emotions. The upshot of all of these different theories and positions is that there is little consensus on a definition of emotion and similarly no agreement on the number of emotion categories. The only real agreement is that emotions are important and impact both mental and bodily health and that they can be implicit in the formation of moods.

Emotion versus Mood

Moods and emotions co-exist. The key difference between emotion and moods is in the duration and intensity of each. Emotions are typically brief (Ekman, 1994) whereas moods are longer, less intense, and may lack awareness of the eliciting stimulus (Elfenbein, 2007). Emotions occur more swiftly in response to a stimulus or perceived occurrence whereas moods may not be tied to a specific event but affect a person's outlook and attitude over a longer time frame. Moods are less important in understanding behavior (Beedie et al., 2005; Scherer, 2005) and may not demand the immediate response that occurs in emotion. A mood may result from an accumulation of factors and thus may not be attributable to a specific happening. This is important within workplace contexts as work events may provoke emotions, but moods may occur from a variety of events including work, home, and family influences. Although moods are entwined with emotions, this chapter is focused mainly on primary emotions and the influence of hybrid work on emotions and the reactions that can ensue from emotions at work.

Emotional Dynamics at Work

Traditionally, researchers and managers used to deny the importance of emotion at work suggesting that employees 'left their emotions at the door' once they entered their place of work. This is a dehumanising fallacy that is impossible to achieve because whether or not they are acknowledged or displayed, emotions occur at work on a daily basis and may be displayed or hidden. Emotions at work are mixed and ambivalent and even unpleasant emotions have valuable roles. The effect of emotion on mood is approximately five times stronger for negative events because negative emotions have a greater functional value such as protecting people from danger, as in the emotion of fear. Negative emotions take more of our cognitive resources to deal with a situation and may explain why they have a stronger impact than positive emotions in many cases. Individual differences play a role as people interpret situations differently and you can improve awareness of your own feelings and responses to emotions which can help you navigate organisational life. Emotional intelligence is increasingly becoming a sought-after workplace skill—or even a superpower that can be vital in decision-making, work actions, and workplace reputation (Kohler, 2023).

People choose their workplace environments and different work environments promote various emotional responses. For example, both the companies I recently researched had created environments that felt exciting, pleasurable, and safe. These were feelings I experienced and recorded as I encountered the bright colours, interesting multi-use spaces, free food and coffee, games, and leisure equipment. There was even a netball hoop in the Gecko company. However, unfortunately some of the most common workplace emotions are anger, frustration, and uncertainty (Kohler, 2023). While anger at work can be motivating, it can also create a lot of stress. Fear and uncertainty can be numbing and demotivating and frustration can cause interpersonal issues between colleagues. An important point to keep in mind about emotions at work is that they are short-lived, temporary states so it may be worth encouraging moderation and regulation of any extreme responses until the emotional state has receded and a more measured, considered reaction is possible.

Some jobs require emotions to be regulated and even faked such as in hospitality roles. Workplaces such as Disneyland promote happiness using the tagline 'the happiest place on earth' as it seeks to promote warmth, joy and happy times for all. Staff in roles that serve others having a good time are expected to regulate their emotions to foster warmth, friendliness, and they often have to display positive emotions as they are considered part of some services. This is a concept known as 'emotional labour' that was originally identified in Arlie Hochschild's (1983) book, *The Managed Heart*. In emotional labour, buffering and neutralising may occur where acceptable emotions are displayed (or faked) in front-of-house interactions and genuine emotions are only permitted in back-of-house or outside the workplace. Sometimes performing a specific emotion such as joyfulness can result in genuinely feeling the emotion (commonly known as 'fake it until you make it') and this is a complex aspect of workplace emotions and 'feeling rules' that determine acceptable emotional displays. Displaying contrary emotion to what we actually feel can create dissonance that over time can cause issues such as alienation from the authentic self. This can be stressful and lead to burnout and anxiety disorders (Brook, 2009; Hochschild, 1983).

Emotions are meant to move us and sometimes an experience triggers an overt response. If responses are too intense for the context people may be perceived as 'out of control' and this is particularly relevant to expressing anger at work. At work we often have to block or mask our desired behavioural responses (display regulation) because responses like anger may be governed by workplace or societal rules and norms (Brook, 2009). Display regulation occurs when the underlying feeling is still present, but people manage or nullify their emotional expressions of a particular feeling. Storing emotions to express in safer situations is a cognitive strategy (e.g. swearing with friends after workplace about a workplace incident), although venting is not always constructive and can feed negative emotions in a group contagion. Practicing potential responses can help to manage strong emotions and considering a range of possible responses can be a useful workplace device.

So, what is the link to hybrid work you might ask? I also asked this question and luckily I had a keen master's student who was interested enough to pursue this question in her research project. She undertook her research within my *Fun and Wellbeing in the Workplace* project. Alexandra Venn-Brown explored the research question: *Has hybrid work had an impact on employee emotions, and if so, how is this significant?*'.

I was enthused to supervise this interesting research work. Happily, Alex has agreed to allow use some of her data extracts in this book and other published work, so I take a moment here to acknowledge her work and thank her for this generous permission. Therefore, extracts used in this in this chapter are from this linked sub-project where participants were asked explicitly about their emotions in hybrid work. The following sections offer three key themes that Alex identified as significant to understanding emotions in hybrid work. They are: (1) varying emotions created by hybrid work, (2) reading emotions, and (3) portraying emotion online.

Emotional Connection, Disconnection, and Everything Between

Hybrid work may evoke a variety of emotions fluctuating between both positive emotions and the more negative or challenging ones. In keeping with the title of this book, happiness is one of the most significant of the positive emotions experienced in hybrid work. Happiness may be experienced when workers enjoy the flexibility and balance that hybrid work offers. This may enhance contentment and workers consistently emphasised how much they enjoy the convenience of working in their own home environment, or alternatively the stimulation of working in a remote location such as their local café, lubricated with a cup of their favourite beverage. Hybrid work can increase worker motivation through a worker's ability to operate autonomously choosing how and where they work, plus there is the affirming recognition that they are trusted by their employer. This feeds into a sense of gratitude for the opportunity to balance work, personal preferences, and family responsibilities. Connectedness may be experienced on the days that workers attend the office and are co-located with colleagues in a shared space such as an office.

However, workers may also experience several negative emotions through feelings of isolation, and they may feel disconnected from colleagues and the workplace community. Stress might be experienced through struggling to balance the boundaries between family responsibilities, home distractions, and work demands. Workers may feel anxious about performance, visibility to managers, and the potential loss of opportunity through feeling unseen when working remotely. Additionally, technology can cause frustration, through miscommunication, misreading tone and body language in online meetings, and the frustration of unplanned offline time, and other technology malfunctions may engender strong negative emotions.

In my own hybrid work, I live a good distance away from my university campus, in a rural beach environment and I feel lucky and grateful to live in a place I experience as a natural paradise. However, we have regular issues with our power supply that cause the internet to stop working. This means that I need to either hotspot from my phone or work offline for stretches of time. One cyclone (Gabrielle) in 2023 wiped out power in my area for five days making working from home very tricky. I do note that the same cyclone caused several tragic deaths throughout my country, so my power outage was insignificant in this wider context. So, you can discern the mixed emotions here—frustration that I could not work combined with the feeling of gratitude for being alive and safe. During the cyclone and the days that followed, power was still available in my university building but the roads that I travel were not passable for a few days. I resorted to visiting my nearest supermarket who offered free Wi-Fi as they had a large generator, and I was able to get messages to work colleagues, after charging my phone from my car. This was an extreme situation that affected my hybrid work and caused some anxiety, but a variety of small, everyday issues can cause different frustrations and anxiety, especially if communication channels are compromised. My personal example highlights that mixed emotions are generated by hybrid work, so people may feel ambivalence about hybrid work where they experience conflicting feelings, often simultaneously. A mixture of positive and negative emotions may be the constant reality of hybrid work.

Below are some responses from the workers that Alex interviewed specifically about their emotions when working in a hybrid format:

> Hybrid…gives you a lot more freedom to do things…in my case, I spend three hours travelling to and from work, maybe even more sometimes, and hybrid frees that up. If I use it productively, I can go do the things I want to do and still have some time to chill. So, like, you know, I can jump out and go for a walk or do things that I would prefer to do rather than travel (Sahil, Auditor).

> I love the face-to-face. But when you're working in an industry where you're constantly getting face to face with customers, you don't always want to have face-to-face with your team members, you need to have the balance. If I had the choice, I would say I like working remotely. I'm self-motivated, I like the people contact, and I contact people where I need to. But when it comes to getting down and actually working without distraction and without the travel, the waste of petrol, and the waste of time. Yeah, I'd work…hybrid, without question (Kate, Business Development Manager).

Both Kate and Sahil outline some key points about emotions in hybrid work. Sahil focuses on his personal freedom and the time he can use more productively when he does not have to commute to his workplace. He also notes that hybrid work allows him to do activities such as going for a walk and this links to the factors of autonomy and work-life balance which are significant aspects of happiness, implying that Sahil is happy in his hybrid work. Kate points to the lack of distraction in remote work but sees the need for balance in maintaining contact with people. She prefers the hybrid work mode, and her response also reinforces the happiness dimensions of autonomy and the social factors of community and belonging.

In our emotions research project, all of the participants emphasised that they wanted the freedom and flexibility of hybrid work so that they could balance their lives and have autonomy over their time—especially in claiming back time that had been previously spent commuting. At the same time, they still valued the social factors of community, belonging, and engaging in organisational cultural events. Their responses accentuated the key happiness factors (outlined in Chapter 1) but participants offered a balanced perspective through their recognition of their own positive and negative emotional reactions.

Decoding Emotional Expression

All participants in Alex's study identified that communication in remote work was difficult due to the loss of physical cues such as eye contact and body language. They linked these missing cues to an issue with interpreting the emotions of colleagues when online, and they all identified negative impacts when emotional cures were missing because this could lead to misinterpretations and of what others were feeling, expressing, and saying. Here are some representative responses:

> [in hybrid work] you're just not sharing as much as you would in person, right? So that connection that you get from sitting in a room and sharing learnings and sharing your feelings, I don't think you keep that in a hybrid type environment. So, I think you do miss out. And it's just that since you're not having that physical element and talking to people, like you're only talking when you have to collaborate on meetings, you're missing out on that personal component…that time in the office. I spend an hour getting to work and I spend an hour coming back from work. But the time that I spend at work, that cross pollination, of information, of sharing of knowledge, of getting to know people and developing relationships, that's lost in that hybrid environment, because…on a zoom call…there's no niceties, there's no getting to know somebody, it's all business, right (Philip, Sales Manager).

> Like if…you're not able to understand their emotion like you've read the emotion wrong, like through text message, or through email, you never know…if you're talking through email or text message…you aren't going to understand their emotion. So, it could be you're reading it that they're angry, but they're just kind of talking normally, or you're reading it that everything's fine, but they're actually getting quite frustrated with you. So,

> I guess you're kind of playing a guessing game or walking on eggshells. Sometimes you might feel like a bit on edge trying to, like, understand an email that's getting quite heated. Whereas you could just walk down to their office and just ask them when physically at work......So it's kind of just leading to unnecessary conflict or confusion. Yeah, it could have been solved in person. Yeah, but it's just like reading the tense, like the tone of how they're talking, which is virtually impossible over just reading words on a screen. So yeah, lots of like, I guess, heightened kind of nerves. Yeah, if you don't want to upset someone, if you're talking to like a boss, you just want to make sure you're on the same page of like, how you're understanding what they're saying (Charlotte, Sports Coordinator).

> It's hard to communicate online. We use Microsoft Teams, where you can't see people's facial expressions or hand gestures or whatever else we use to communicate. Without those, like visual prompts, you might perceive a message wrong, like someone might just be trying to tell you something, and you might take it as like, it was rude, it just really depends on how a person communicates over messages (Sahil, Auditor).

> Face-to-face...I can kind of read the room, I can kind of understand where the person's at, I can understand the body language. And I think you miss all of that in...hybrid. You know, that's one of the things that I kind of find... you miss out on picking up all of those cues, right? Body language, eye contact, focus... you miss out on all of those cues, where if you were sitting in the room, you kind of understand now I need to kind of move on...they've lost interest (Philip, Sales Manager).

> And that's very hard if you are...sat behind the desk, and you're dealing with this remotely. But when you see how they sit at their desk and how they fix themselves a cup of coffee, you can tell if there's an issue. Yeah, and you're missing that in online work when you're working remotely. You can't see those physical elements, not all of them. Yeah, it's just harder behind screens (Kate, Business Development Manager).

Note the anxiety and tensions experienced by these participants as they worry about not fully understanding the emotions of others. They suggest that emotions are less visible behind a screen or in textual communications such as messages and emails. Philip, a manager, suggests that the social aspects of the workplace get lost in hybrid work because screen meetings are 'all business' without the niceties of human interaction. Charlotte emphasises that online communication can upset people through miscommunication, and Sahil also is concerned over perceiving an online message incorrectly. Philip and Kate both mention body language and how that can assist interpreting emotional response, and they recognise that it is missing in online messaging which makes communication harder.

The anxiety of misperception seems a key factor for these workers as they grapple with how to interpret the emotions of colleagues when communicating via technology. So, these participants have raised two significant emotional aspects—a low-level anxiety experienced through reading the emotions of others onscreen and the possibility of misinterpretation, alongside an inference that reading emotions is important in the workplace and happens more easily in face-to-face forms of communication. This would suggest that some work activities are better suited to being co-located in the same space and other activities that require concentration and avoiding distraction, are well-suited to online communications. It is interesting to note that the social aspects of emotions at work were highlighted because this is not always considered or managed when companies encourage or permit hybrid work.

Letting Emotions Show

Alex's emotion interviews were semi-structured, offering participants the opportunity to debate interesting points, discuss aspects that were important to them and to share information that might not have been asked for in the pre-prepared questions. This flexibility generated this final interesting theme on emotional display, and it arose as a result of participants' articulating their own thought-provoking points about displaying emotion, the importance of this, and different ways to achieve this in hybrid work.

Below, Sahil notes variations in communication styles and reveals his own preference for being less expressive through simply commenting 'sweet' to show his pleasure and happiness. He indicates that a more expressive and impassioned colleague might write their response in all capital letters (in a textual exchange) and this is highly expressive because using 'all caps' denotes shouting in text messages and emails.

> In hybrid work you have to try to communicate, and everyone communicates differently and receives things differently. So, I guess, communicating over strictly just messages and grammar, how punctual people are in

> their messages can be open to interpretation…if communicating on the computer and I was happy with something I'd be like 'sweet', whereas someone might be like, overly expressive, like, all caps or something (Sahil, Auditor).

> If you're talking through email or text message with someone, you're not able to, unless you use lots of emojis and exclamation marks, you are not going to get your emotion across. And then vice versa, you aren't going to understand their emotion (Charlotte, Sports Coordinator).

Charlotte identifies the importance of using emojis and exclamation marks to display emotions as emojis are a short-hand way of inserting an emotive response into a text. Emojis are icons or small symbols that can represent emotions, objects, and ideas. They add expressions to text communications that can suggest tone and feelings. They also add fun and visual interest to messages and there is a huge range of emojis available on emoji toolbars that make their insertion seamless in word processing applications. Charlotte notes that emojis are important and she suggests that emotion will not be conveyed unless you use these inserted devices. However, popular advice regarding the use of emojis cautions against overusing them, which can be distracting and seem unprofessional in workplace communication. Therefore, emojis should perhaps be only used just to highlight a significant emotion or point within well-established collegial relationships.

Further to these points, Sahil notes that using emojis and devices such as ALL CAPS would make him feel vulnerable and anxious. He would rather not employ any emotional cues in his technological communication and notes that he can also be his true self when he is working alone as he does not need to display his emotions to colleagues.

> I'd feel very vulnerable and anxious knowing these people know what I've communicated and how I'm feeling. And then if it's not being taken into account, I don't think I'd feel good at all…Yeah, instead of worrying about what people would think if I was [being emotional], I probably wouldn't

react. Because I wouldn't want to give off any impression. You get to be your true self if you're by yourself (Sahil, Auditor).

The participant responses clarify the importance of individual preferences when displaying emotion in hybrid work, both in face-to-face communication and in textual communication via email or messaging. A professional tone is usually a safe option, and communication should be calm and respectful. Devices such as punctuation or emojis can help to suggest a positive tone, appreciation or enthusiasm. Overemoting can be perceived as too informal or unprofessional so emojis and rhetorical devices should be used sparingly and appropriately. It is advisable to understand the context and the relationship between those involved in exchanges because different situations require different types and levels of emotion. Personally, I never use an emoji when conveying bad or upsetting news, (something I'd always prefer to do in person) as it can suggest flippancy, casualness, and insensitivity rather than conveying empathy and care.

BACK-TO-THE-OFFICE MANDATES

As I was writing this book the landscape for work began to change with back-to-the-office mandates being imposed by management on many global workers and it seems to be a highly emotive and important issue. For many workers hybrid work has become an established norm and they relish the flexibility that this confers, many now considering this as a necessity to balance their increasingly busy lives. While hybrid work has been embraced and normalised, most recently the media has reported that back—to-the-office mandates are being enforced around the world, and this has resulted in some strong reactions and emotions from employees that consider this short-sighted and unacceptable. Such mandates have caused turnover, decreased engagement, and fostered discontent among groups of workers. In October 2024 Amazon initiated a return-to-office mandate that according to Forbes, left 91% of workers dissatisfied, with 73% looking for new jobs. Other large companies are following suit (Boeing, Goldman Sachs, UPS and Dell for example) and critics argue that these mandates represent an outdated approach to management because modern workers have multiple needs and responsibilities that require flexibility. These new regimes are creating a decline in morale through invoking feelings of resentment and dissatisfaction. These mandates also imply a loss of trust in workers and those workers that do not resign may feel trapped and disengaged and may decrease their effort resulting in lower performance and productivity. All of these factors may cause long-lasting damage to organisational culture.

I encountered a new term when researching the recent back-to-the-office mandates and this is the notion of 'coffee badging'. Coffee badging is the practice of showing up at the office to establish that you were physically present for just long enough to have coffee and interact socially with colleagues and then leaving to work from home. This implies workers are still keen to socialise, but it also highlights the friction between those wanting flexible, hybrid work and authority figures pushing for a return to the physical office. Coffee badging is a way of skirting the rules and it is not ideal as it still involves a commute time for the worker and suggests that the emerging back-to-the-office practices do not best accommodate workers' needs for flexible work arrangements. After all, many workers may feel that they quickly pivoted to hybrid and remote work when Covid lockdowns required this and proved that they could still perform successfully in this mode of work. Hardly surprising that resentment may now arise when this has option has been summarily revoked by management now that the crisis has eased. One solution might be to offer free coffee at work within social sessions where workers can enjoy drinking it with groups of colleagues, hopefully enticing workers to stay in the office afterwards. However, the fact that coffee badging has emerged suggests a resistance from workers required to return to in-office work after they have enjoyed the benefits of flexible, hybrid work. This emerging trend, seen by many workers as regressive, demonstrates the highly emotional aspects tied to hybrid work where workers that may have been happy with their freedom and flexibility now experience resentment or even anger, if this option is overturned.

Autonomy: The Key to Hybrid Happiness

Research, online blogs, reports, and our recent emotion research findings all align on one key fact: having the freedom to work in a hybrid way fosters workplace happiness for most workers. This is attributed to the autonomy it grants, the reduction in commuting time, and the ability to achieve work-life balance in personalised ways. Most significantly, the symbolic aspect of hybrid work is that it implies management and organisational trust in the individual worker perhaps even generating reciprocity in the form of extra work effort and commitment to the company.

Back-to-the-office mandates are not proving popular with workers who have had 4–5 years to get used to a more flexible hybrid work mode, where they choose some days in the office and some working from home. This shift is stimulating emotional responses such as resentment and promoting new behaviors like coffee-badging as a form of resistance to the loss of freedom and flexibility. Hybrid work is emotional, and all of the workers interviewed reinforced this, outlining multiple different nuanced emotions, ranging from frustration and anxiety to positive feelings. The most significant point emphasised by hybrid workers was that flexibility, autonomy and trust generated well-being and happiness.

REFERENCES

Amazon is 'taking a risk' with its five-day return-to-office plans, experts say. Retrieved February 18, 2025, from https://www.raconteur.net/future-of-work/amazon-return-to-office-plans

Beedie, C., Terry, P., & Lane, A. (2005). Distinctions between emotion and mood. *Cognition and Emotion, 19*(6), 847–878.

Brook, P. (2009). The Alienated Heart: Hochschild's 'emotional labour' thesis and the anticapitalist politics of alienation. *Capital & Class, 33*(2), 7–31.

Coffee Badging Is A New Workplace Trend For Hybrid Workers—Here's Why It May Be A Good Thing. Retrieved February 19, 2025, from https://www.msn.com/en-us/health/wellness/coffee-badging-is-a-new-workplace-trend-for-hybrid-workers-here-s-why-it-may-be-a-good-thing/ar-AA1wa6EJ?ocid=BingNewsVerp

Cooper, C. L., & Cartwright, S. (2001). Organizational management of stress and destructive emotions at work. *Emotions at work: theory, research and applications for management* (pp. 269–280).

Debate around hybrid and WFH arrangements persists amid ongoing push to return to office—ABC News. Retrieved February 19, 2025, from https://www.abc.net.au/news/2025-02-10/nsw-work-from-home-office-hybrid-arrangements-families-parents/104872232

Ekman, P. (1994). *Moods, emotions, and traits.* Fundamental Questions, Oxford University Press.

Elfenbein, H. A. (2007). 7 Emotion in organizations: A review and theoretical integration. *The Academy of Management Annals, 1*(1), 315–386.

Frijda, N. H. (1986). *The emotions.* Cambridge University Press.

Hochschild, A. R. (1983). *The managed heart. Commercialization of human feeling*. University of California Press.
How Return To Office Policies Are Impacting Employees In 2024. Retrieved February 19, 2025, from https://www.forbes.com/sites/karadennison/2024/07/10/how-return-to-office-policies-are-impacting-employees-in-2024/
Kohler, L. (2023). Why your emotions are your work superpower. Forbes. Retrieved February 19, 2025, from https://www.forbes.com/sites/lindsaykohler/2023/08/30/why-your-emotions-are-your-work-superpower/
Scherer, K. R. (2005). What are emotions? And how can they be measured? *Social Science Information, 44*(4), 695–729.
Solo and hybrid work: Navigating our future and new normal. Retrieved February 19, 2025, from https://www.bbc.com/reel/video/p09p4p1r/solo-and-hybrid-work-navigating-our-future-and-new-normal
The Real Impact Of Return-To-Office Mandates On Productivity At Work. Retrieved February 18, 2025, from https://www.forbes.com/sites/carolinecastrillon/2024/10/06/impact-of-return-to-office-mandates-on-productivity/
What Is Coffee Badging, and Why Is It Mostly Men Doing It?. Retrieved February 19, 2025, from https://tech.co/news/what-is-coffee-badging-men
2025 HR trends: the agentic workplace, DEI 3.0 and HR's rebrand—Raconteur. Retrieved February 18, 2025, from https://www.raconteur.net/talent-culture/2025-hr-trends?utm_source=Sailthru&utm_medium=email&utm_campaign=Raconteur%20Daily&utm_term=daily-newsletter

CHAPTER 6

Being Happy and Hybrid

HAPPINESS

Happiness is considered to be a positive emotional state that includes feelings of contentment, satisfaction, joy, and fulfilment. It is linked to well-being in various life aspects such as relationships, experiences, and accomplishments. Seeing happiness as an important aspect of humanity is an ancient idea dating back to moral philosophers such as Aristotle, Epicurus, Socrates and Plato. Aristotle argued that happiness is the highest desire and ambition for a person that can be reached through cultivating virtue within oneself. In effect, he argued that happiness was not a fleeting pleasure but comes from a life well-lived. Epicurus believed that happiness arises from simple pleasures and argued that balance and temperance generate space for happiness. He prioritised a minimalist lifestyle and saw friendship as most important to happiness. Socrates and Plato equated happiness with virtue and argued that living a just life that emphasises truth and reason is the key to happiness (Sus, 2024).

Modern philosophers such as Kant argued that moral living creates inner peace, resulting in happiness whereas Nietzsche saw happiness as self-growth and power. Existentialists argue that happiness is not guaranteed because life is absurd, but it may be achieved through meaningful choices (Weller, 2016).

Happiness is composed of several key constructs including feelings of joy and pleasure (affective well-being), a sense of meaning and purpose

© The Author(s), under exclusive license to Springer Nature
Singapore Pte Ltd. 2025
B. Plester, *Hybrid Happiness*,
https://doi.org/10.1007/978-981-95-2092-3_6

in life (eudaimonic well-being) and life satisfaction related to well-being (Steptoe, 2019). Overall, happiness is not considered to be a state of constant euphoria but a sense of experiencing more positive emotions than negative ones. Martin Seligman (2018) is one of the founders of the positive psychology movement and he developed the acronym PERMA to represent five elements of happiness which are:

1. Positive emotions
2. Engagement
3. Relationships
4. Meaning
5. Accomplishment

Seligman argues that each of the five PERMA elements has to contribute to happiness and well-being, and each element is equally important and is measured independently from the others. The five elements in the model are considered to be intrinsically motivating and the model considers happiness to be both pleasure-based (hedonic) and meaning-based (eudaimonic). The value in the PERMA model is that it has a focus on the positive aspects of life which can be empowering, contrasting with traditional psychological models that focus on harmful conditions such as trauma, depression, and anxiety. PERMA can give people some defined areas to work on within their different life contexts, including the workplace. Overarchingly, the model encourages a holistic perspective on happiness that suggests that when a person can balance the combination of these five elements, they will experience more happiness. The concept of happiness is frequently used interchangeably with subjective well-being (Farooq et al., 2024) which will be further discussed in a later section.

Happiness at Work

Since most people spend much of their lives at work, and because happiness is defined by how people evaluate their whole lives, work plays a significant role in shaping happiness for workers around the world (de Neve and Ward, 2017). Some companies pay for happiness coaches and consultants (Misra & Srivastava, 2022). High profile companies such as

Google, Deloitte, TikTok, EY and Coca Cola have even appointed executive roles dedicated to prioritising happiness and boosting morale (Kelly, 2024) creating job titles such as Chief Happiness Officer (CHO). CEO of happiness—or CHO—may be my new favourite job title!

Happiness at work can be divided into physical factors and psychological factors. Physical factors include a good salary, being able to afford goods such as a house and/or car and includes factors such as job characteristics, and physical workplace conditions. Psychological aspects include skill development, interesting challenges, achievement opportunities, a sense of belonging, organisational pride, relationships, and a sense of meaning in ones' work (Misra & Srivastava, 2022). A recent workplace study identified these key factors that drive happiness at work:

- Supportive leadership and positive relationships with supervisors
- Autonomy and a sense of control over one's work
- Opportunities for growth, learning, and recognition
- Work-life balance and psychological safety (Jaswal et al., 2024)

These factors align with key points in this book from earlier chapters and also with the responses from research participants gathered from interviews about fun and humour where they offered information about happiness in their work context. Here are five examples of the things they saw as important to their happiness at work. Please be aware, there are two partially repeated extracts in this section (Andy and Irene) but they illustrate points about happiness here whereas they exemplified different points in earlier chapters. The first short extract is a short part of an extract presented earlier in Chapter 4—but is worth offering again as it makes an important link between fun, trust, and happiness, for Andy whose job focuses on staff well-being. The second repeated section is Irene's comment about the physical work environment, which was seen in Chapter 3 as an example of workplace artefacts, whereas here the focus is on how this makes her happy:

> Because happiness for me is that you have fun while you're at work, you trust the people you work with (Andy, Firefly).

> And the moment I walk into the building, as you can see all these colours, does make you feel happy. It has a very important psychological effect. You know, you see this and then you see fun. And as you see the green

house, we have like the set up with all of the you know, fairy lights. And it's beautiful that the balloons were for, like a celebration, but are not normally there. But the fairy lights are and all of these colour palettes. I don't know who designed it, but it's brilliant. So, it gives you that feeling of energy and fun (Irene, Firefly).

There are a lot of different people practices in Gecko that make, make it like a happy place to work. Like - makes you feel like - oh yeah, it's a good employer that takes care of me (Vlad, Gecko).

I already feel like - like Marnie and the People & Culture team they are doing such a good job keeping everyone entertained and keeping everyone happy. So other than that, I mean bringing the netball hoop into the office was something that I would never think about (laughter). And we also like to play games, and we play music, and we just have a good time (laughter) (Fiona, Gecko).

I would say, if I were to think about it I would say feeling happy and feeling accomplished. Yes, and then just like you know the feeling of what I want to do - I've done that. So having my own clear objectives and then you know achieving those. Just some things that I've achieved and feeling content. So that's like a - you know - if I'm doing - if I have that - then I'm *well* (Nihal, Gecko).

There are a variety of factors that make these workers happy—as represented in their comments. The ability to have fun at work and trusting people are important to Andy who also talks about psychological safety (see Chapter 4) at Firefly that enables fun and trust to occur. Andy a senior manager in the People and Culture team, also further articulated that he assumes responsibility to offer these values to others in the company. Vlad mentions 'people practices' and notes that his workplace is a happy one which makes him feel cared for by his employer, while Fiona gives credit to the People and Culture team for keeping the workforce happy. She illustrates the new netball hoop in the office as an example of the company encouraging play, noting how games and music contribute to workplace happiness at Gecko. Irene focuses upon the bright colours of her workplace where all the walls are painted with positive uplifting slogans in bright script creating a sense of fun and energising her. She also talks about sections of the office decorated permanently with fairy lights—I also noticed this during my time there. There was a house-shaped A-frame festooned with fairy lights that created a type of sparkly grotto and meetings were held within this space on comfortable chairs and beanbags, creating a relaxed and fun ambience that felt happy and playful.

My research shows that key drivers of happiness at work involve prioritising social bonds through interesting initiatives (such as the netball hoop at Gecko) and ensuring that workers feel cared for and safe to enjoy themselves. It is important that workers experience accomplishment, receive recognition, and feel appreciated. Office design is also important with consideration given to light and quiet spaces, and/or bright energising displays and distinctive spaces. At the same time flexibility in work is becoming increasingly important to workers' happiness and so while office spaces are important, so too is the freedom to enjoy hybrid work by working in the office space and also remotely. People and Culture teams seem to play an important role in helping create workplace happiness. Because many of the positive actions and processes involved with happiness are closely linked to well-being, this is outlined next.

Workplace Well-Being

During my research I asked workers specific questions about well-being and what it meant for them in relation to their work. Well-being is part of happiness as it incorporates positive emotions such as contentment, achievement, purposeful and meaningful activities, and maintaining positive relationships in work and home life. There are many well-being studies, mostly in psychology and they identify multiple dimensions that create psychological well-being. One of the early influential, landmark models is Carol Ryff's (1989) six-dimensional model contending that these factors constitute psychological well-being:

1. autonomy
2. environmental mastery
3. personal growth
4. positive relations with others
5. purpose in life
6. self-acceptance

This model shifted the focus of well-being from simply feeling well to incorporate functioning well as a person. Similar to the PERMA happiness model, this model brings in the eudaimonic aspects of well-being which are those linked with purpose and personal development rather than prioritising fleeting happiness. It is an enduring and holistic model of wellbeing that is one of the most cited models in positive psychology and there is much overlap with the psychological model of happiness—so combining both offers a multi-dimensional understanding of ways in which people flourish at work.

The workers that discussed workplace well-being in my research all had the option to work in a hybrid model with one exception—Daisy at Gecko worked as receptionist so was expected to be onsite five days a week. She did, however, feel that she could manage to achieve personal well-being in her office-based role even though all of her colleagues could choose hybrid work. In the extracts below, several of the well-being dimensions are cited as workers talk about the flexibility and autonomy in hybrid work (Jasper), purpose in their work as well as physical, mental, and spiritual aspects to their well-being (Jack and Daisy). Dev, the Gecko founder, mentions fun as part of well-being, Vlad identifies balance as important, and Andy talks about finding ways to help his workers ensure well-being at work, mentioning resources, guidance, and help with mental well-being.

> I'm able to do hybrid work. I do have a lot that requires me to be here. Um, I like to be here four to five days… but I just come in later - leave later - or work from home for the first part [of the day]. So, it's - we are adults - quite flexible. It's just strictly the traffic to be honest, because that's …yeah, tell me about it. It's completely changed how people can balance work and life. I mean, there's a reason I keep coming back. And I've stuck around here, even though I'm supposed to be a millennial who changes jobs? It's because this place um that's, um, I mean, at the very least, it's very safe. You know, it's good to me (Jasper, Firefly).

> I think well-being is just a, probably a state of balance. Somewhere - where, I guess, like, balance in all things, sort of, like, I guess, spiritual, mental, physical. I think that would be what well-being is - is kind of having all those pillars in your life in, like, an equal state so that you feel content. In order for me to be in a state of well-being I know that I also need to have a strong self-discipline in order to do the things that, you know, may

not be immediately contributing to my well-being... I would say my well-being more comes from, sort of, being satisfied in the work I'm doing and fulfilling, like, my role and having a purpose in the company (Jack, Gecko).

I think well-being for me is... for me well-being is a lot more about mental clarity than it is about physical. Because, I feel like, if you're mentally not there you physically won't be there either...if I'm supported mentally - I'm physically, I'm not tired, and things like that. So, I think a lot of well-being for me is that kind of, like, rather than being, like, eat apples or fruit...[well-being] comes from having - being in the right head space... compared to other employers that I've worked for, I definitely think this place provides a lot of support for well-being (Daisy, Gecko).

I think you can describe all of the other aspects about anxiety and stress and all of those things. But if everything's properly balanced, I feel like it results in health and motivation to do things. And that doesn't necessarily only mean work... For me, going to work, a big part of it is enjoyment, being around people. I'm a little Gen-E - I like to - I like to have fun - I like to take long breaks, yeah, have a long lunch, go for a walk, things like that (Dev, Founder, Gecko).

[Well-being] for me that means having a balanced life where you have a good amount of rest and fun and work. And as well, as well as - well I guess that that quite describes that but there are of course other aspects of that such as, you know, being in the moment, enjoying the - the - present, presence, where you are at now (Vlad, Gecko).

Well-being is a big part of my role. And it's a big part. But it's understanding really, because I think everybody's idea of well-being is different. You can talk to consultants who will say, 'we'll do this well-being survey' - they will talk to, you know, other providers who will give you a snippet of well-being and I just wish there was somebody who just thought about the whole the full breadth of well-being and how we make a difference is much wider scale doesn't mean how we feel like we did we do little pockets of stuff...maybe I just need to give people resources where they can - where they can look after that themselves and take control of their own well-being - be responsible for their own well-being... ...we talk about, you know, making people aware of what mental well-being you know, and offering resources for people suffering ...offering, you know, advice and guidance (Andy, Firefly).

Well-being is often one of the reasons that hybrid work is permitted and is seen as one of the major benefits, but researchers advise that it is a complex relationship (Dale et al., 2024). Having the flexibility to work in a hybrid model can improve sleep and nutrition (Franklin, 2023), allow workers more leisure time, and may increase energy levels while reducing tiredness (Montreuil & Lippel, 2003). The increased autonomy in hybrid work can benefit psychological health and contribute to positive well-being (Li et al., 2023). Overall, hybrid work improves well-being through the ability to balance work, caring obligations, and domestic activities resulting in better home lives for workers. However, working from home has been associated with more sedentary behaviour, the extension of work hours (Parry et al., 2021) and work intensification which can result in mental and physical health detriments (Hunt & Pickard, 2022). Workers may actually overwork themselves through working longer working hours, as they may struggle to establish a clear end to their workday. Additionally, workers may not have an ideal ergonomic setup at their home which can result in physical discomfort or health issues over time. Therefore, if hybrid work is permitted, managers and organisational leaders need to help their workers to achieve an optimal balance so that the benefits of hybrid work are achieved and this includes both physical and psychological aspects of work.

Well-Being without Walls

Happiness and well-being concepts are both typified by the notion of balance in life. The idea of balance is an important part of successful hybrid work. The key to achieving happiness in hybrid work is through blending flexibility and autonomy with high-level communication and connection with co-workers. Hybrid work can reduce stress, anxiety, and burnout compared to full in-office participation. The flexibility of hybrid work may improve well-being through creating personal harmony. Hybrid models allow people to control their work to align with their personal rhythms which can involve avoiding long commutes or working at times they feel at their peak and focused. This autonomy can improve sleep, allow workers to develop healthier routines, and free-up more time for family, sport, or hobbies. Lucia outlines this as she describes when her company changed the hybrid model to allow two or three days WFH and this made her happy as it aligns with her life and activities:

Well, last year, for example, it was at the beginning when we were trialling this hybrid mode. It was a bit more strict and it was more, like, you need to have a company day, you need to have a team day, and a personal day and it was a bit more strict. And, that didn't help, but at the same time we did a survey, and they listened that we were happier with two days instead of three days. So, 'cause I do remember, who was it? I think it was Lydia, she came around and she was, like, really happy and she was, like, have you heard? We can come two days now, not three (laughter). So, I do the Tuesday - the company day and then I do Thursdays because Wednesdays I go to spinning class and it's slightly earlier. And I need to get there on time (laughter). So, all of that - it really helps for, like, you were asking before the wellbeing …Because it just fits really well in my life in general…with all the other activities that I have (Lucia, Gecko).

As discussed earlier in the book, trust and culture are important for well-functioning hybrid teams and companies that trust employees to manage their time and offer support rather than surveillance are likely to have happier, more engaged workers. Hybrid work can become a representation of mutual respect and shared accountability. With this mindset, hybrid work is not simply a logistical shift but a cultural one that empowers people to thrive both professionally and personally. Hybrid work models exemplify a balanced approach—activating the autonomy of remote work while keeping the structure and communal benefits of office-based interactions. If optimal conditions are developed, maintained, and regularly evaluated by workers and managers together, then hybrid work models can be a significant factor contributing to workers' holistic well-being and happiness.

Happiness Hacks

It is important when in the remote work phase of hybrid work to ensure that workers remember to take breaks, ensuring that they can access mental health support, and are working in a balanced way with a clear finish time, in order to prevent burnout. Boundaries should be recognised and teams can promote respect for personal time by not sending messages outside of working hours (unless it is really urgent). Team engagement is important and should continue to be fostered using virtual team-building activities and both online and in-person social events will help to strengthen relationships. Recognition and appreciation are important and 'shout outs' or small rewards that regularly recognise and appreciate team members' contributions will help boost morale and maintain positive team dynamics. These practices can be developed and fostered through setting clear expectations for communication etiquette, response times, and the selection and use of appropriate communication channels.

My happiest moments come from spending time with family, playing golf, and walking on the beach with my two big dogs (you met Bowie in Chapter 2—his brother is Fergus—a shaggy, reddish-brown rescue dog). I enjoy and schedule time for reformer pilates sessions in the early mornings, I like to paint and draw and I frequently complete complex 1000-piece puzzles on my dining room table. All of these activities are enabled by hybrid work on the days when I can work from home. Also, when my 60–90minute commute each way is taken out of my day I am left with more time for my leisure pursuits. I punctuate long spells of writing at my desk, with taking a few minutes to put some pieces in the current puzzle or by taking a short walk. Taking mini breaks like this refreshes me and suddenly ideas spring into my mind or a problem gets solved in my brain while I am not actively thinking about it. I have some of my best academic ideas while painting or walking on the beach.

I play golf—a game that I love fiercely but am sure that I will never master. I am what is known as a 'weekend warrior' because I work full-time during the week and most of my golf occurs in the weekends. Many others are in the same boat; thus, my local golf course gets quite busy at the weekends. Hybrid work allows me extra time for golf during the week. New Zealand operates daylight saving time giving us more daylight time to do activities during our spring/summer months from late September until early April. I can work all day (writing this book for example) and I may start at 7 am and then stop around 3–4 pm and head to the golf course for 9 holes of my favourite sport before dark. For me, this offers great stress relief, yes—even when I have found all of the course bunkers and posted a higher score than I'm happy with! Swinging a club, thinking about angles, laughing with my golf buddies all take my focus off work and contribute to my well-being, as does the brisk walk amongst trees, birds, and a tidal estuary nestled beside the course. Hybrid work gives me this and allows me the flexibility to enjoy my favourite game while still being productive at work. Added to this I have days on campus where I meet with colleagues, teach students, attend research sessions, and make the most of in-person contact. I feel that I am truly blending fun, happiness, and work making all of these aspects more enjoyable and reducing work-life stress.

I view this as a privilege and am thankful for my university, my faculty and department leaders for facilitating and permitting my hybrid work mode. Writing this book was a significant undertaking while still completing all of my other academic tasks and responsibilities but being able to work in hybrid mode gave me the space and flexibility to complete this project. Additionally, I was enacting the very thing that I was writing about so that gave the process extra poignancy and relevance as I blended my research work, on-going online engagement, and my own workday experiences into this work. Finding the small moments of fun and pleasure, the little tweaks and hacks that offer breaks and refreshments from keyboard slog, having the space and time to exercise, breathe, ponder and think—these are the well-being benefits and practices that are supported by hybrid work. I know that I have been lucky enough to genuinely experience hybrid happiness, and I hope that you can too.

REFERENCES

Dale, G., Wilson, H., & Tucker, M. (2024). What is healthy hybrid work? Exploring employee perceptions on well-being and hybrid work arrangements. *International Journal of Workplace Health Management, 17*(4), 335–352.

De Neve, J. E., & Ward, G. (2017). Happiness at work—LSE Research Online. Retrieved July 10, 2025, from https://eprints.lse.ac.uk/83604/

Farooq, F., Mohammad, S. S., Nazir, N. A., & Shah, P. A. (2024). Happiness at work: A systematic literature review. *International Journal of Organisational Analysis, 32*(10), 2236–2255.

Franklin, N. (2023). Hybrid workers exercise more, sleep longer and eat better. *Insight*. Retrieved July 10, 2025, from https://workplaceinsight.net/hybrid-workers-exercise-more-sleep-longer-and-eat-better/

Giménez-Nadal, J. I., Molina, J. A., & Velilla, J. (2020). Work time and well-being for workers at home: Evidence from the American Time Use Survey. *International Journal of Manpower, 41*(2), 184–206.

Happiness: What It Really Means and How to Find It. https://www.verywellmind.com/what-is-happiness-4869755

Hunt, T., & Pickard, H. (2022). Harder, better, faster, stronger? Work intensity and 'good work' in the United Kingdom. *Industrial Relations Journal, 53*(3), 189–206.

Jaswal, N., Sharma, D., Bhardwaj, B., & Kraus, S. (2024). Promoting well-being through happiness at work: A systematic literature review and future research agenda. *Management Decision, 62*(13), 332–369.

Kelly, C. (2024). Introducing To The C-Suite: The 'Chief Happiness Officer'. *Forbes*. Retrieved June 30, 2025, from https://www.forbes.com/sites/jackkelly/2024/03/18/introducing-to-the-c-suite-the-chief-happiness-officer/

Li, M., Fu, N., Chadwick, C., & Harney, B. (2023). Untangling human resource management and employee wellbeing relationships: Differentiating job resource HR practices from challenge demand HR practices. *Human Resource Management Journal, 34*(1), 214–235. https://doi.org/10.1111/1748-8583.12527

Misra, N., & Srivastava, S. (2022). Happiness at work: a psychological perspective. In F. Irtelli & F. Gabrielli (Eds.), *Happiness and Wellness* (pp. 95–110).

Montreuil, S., & Lippel, K. (2003). Telework and occupational health: A Quebec empirical study and regulatory implications. *Safety Science, 41*(4), 339–358. https://doi.org/10.1016/s0925-7535(02)00042-5

Parry J, Young Z, Bevan S, Veliziotis M, Baruch Y, Beigi M, Bajorek Z, Salter E, & Tochia C. (2021). Working from Home under Covid-19 Lockdown. *Economic & Social Research Council* (ESRC).

Ryff, C. D. (1989). Happiness is everything, or is it? Explorations on the meaning of psychological well-being. *Journal of Personality and Social Psychology, 57*(6), 1069.

Seligman, M. (2018). PERMA and the building blocks of well-being. *The Journal of Positive Psychology, 13*(4), 333–335.

Steptoe, A. (2019). Happiness and health. *Annual Review of Public Health, 40*(1), 339–359.

Sus, V. (2024). How Did Philosophers of Different Eras Perceive Happiness? *The Collector*. Retrieved July 10, 2025, from https://www.thecollector.com/how-philosophers-perceive-happiness/

The Future of the Office Has Arrived: It's Hybrid. https://www.gallup.com/workplace/511994/future-office-arrived-hybrid.aspx

Unlocking Employee Happiness and Engagement with Hybrid Work | Psychology Today. https://www.psychologytoday.com/us/blog/intentional-insights/202408/unlocking-employee-happiness-and-engagement-with-hybrid-work

Weller, C. (2016). 13 great philosophers on the secret of happiness. *Business Insider*. World Economic Forum. Retrieved July 10, 2025, from https://www.weforum.org/stories/2016/06/13-great-philosophers-on-the-secret-of-happiness/

CHAPTER 7

Tech-Powered Freedom

Tech that Works Where You Do

Technology is essential to making hybrid work successful. As hybrid work has become embedded in many organisations, technological tools are constantly improving, and virtual office spaces may recreate workplace access that feels as if an employee is in the office. There is an increasing selection of tools to foster well-being and engagement with multiple apps available to manage stress and foster positive mental health. Communication tools such as video-conferencing tools facilitate online meetings and offer face-to-face interaction even though colleagues may be physically distant. These include platforms such as Teams, Zoom, and Google Meet as well as messaging tools with chat functions and interactive online platforms such as Slack, Discord, and Rocket.Chat. Sometimes meeting participants use more than one of these tools at the same time, such as when they are instant messaging work friends while an online meeting is in progress. Cloud computing allows easy collaboration and file sharing from any location. Secure virtual private networks (VPNs) and cyber-security help to keep company resources and information safe while AI can help with scheduling, data analysis, and content generation. There is a variety of ergonomic office hardware such as standing desks, portable monitors, and noise cancelling headsets that can help set up the remote work environment for better performance.

Future tools may include augmented and virtual reality tools for immersive remote meetings and automation tools are constantly being developed and improved. Kim (below) notes the changes in technology and believes her current role is truly a hybrid role as the technology has improved and supports her working this way.

> I've had a lot of hybrid roles ...And in fact, hybrid role is very, very interesting, because it's never a term that was used, I have always worked, pretty much since 1992, I've worked in a hybrid role. And really, because of the location of the role that I was working with... because of the remote nature of our job, it was like one day in the office, in fact, the least amount of time you spend in the office, the better. It wasn't like now where we were given - we didn't have the technology to dial-in and I have what's now known as a truly hybrid role (Kim healthcare worker, extract from Alexandra's study).

The Trials and Tribulations of Tech

While tools are improving and making technologically supported remote/hybrid work more successful, there are still many issues associated with relying on technology to work. Some of these have been discussed in earlier chapters dealing with issues such as isolation, connectedness, and team bonding, among others. Some of the specific challenges that are implicitly technological need further elucidation and discussion. The most significant of these is communication and the opportunity for miscommunication to occur. Text-based communication is not always clear and textual communication lacks vocal tone or body language so it can result in messages being misinterpreted or a tone perceived that was not actually intended. As discussed in Chapter 5, text-based communication does not convey emotions as effectively as in-person communication and nuance can be missing sometimes causing misunderstandings and even offence. In face-to-face communication, misunderstandings can be quickly sorted out, but this might take longer in text messages and may not even be addressed at all, leaving communicators with different perceptions of what was intended.

Other issues are the possible over-reliance on technology because any technology can be disrupted by poor internet connectivity, glitches in software, and platform issues. Additionally, it can seem like workers are always having to learn new technologies to keep up to date. I know that this is a significant pressure in my university where it sometimes seems that I have just achieved mastery of a technology platform or software when a new version arrives, resulting in me having to make changes and learn new ways of operating. This can create frustration and delays when dealing with my everyday workload. Training is usually offered for big upgrades or new software, but finding time to complete trainings can be challenging in a full workload where you just want to get on with things. Training itself is usually conducted online but at times I would really prefer to do this in person so that I can stop the process, ask questions, and work through the changes with a knowledgeable person. These processes somehow feel more difficult in online training and it can be very tempting to turn off the mic and camera and do other tasks while ostensibly participating in training sessions – come on you know you have done it!

Data security can be an issue when working from home or remotely as unsecured networks can increase the risk of data breaches and compliance with data protection regulations may be difficult in remote work. Potential issues such as this may need to be negotiated between the worker and the company. In hybrid models, it may be possible to vary the types of work between different locations—for example, using high risk data that needs to stay secured might be work that is done in the office with remote work constituting less sensitive back-up work or administration. Technological solutions such as using a Virtual Private Network (VPN) may be one way of ensuring security in online work.

THE POWER OF TRUST

Trust is an interpersonal social resource that influences behaviour and worker performance, and it influences key work dynamics such as cooperation, problem-solving, and innovation (van Zoonen et al., 2024). It can be defined as a belief in the character, capabilities, and veracity of another person and is considered a cornerstone for interpersonal relationships and is the foundation for successful organisations (Lewis, 2025). As mentioned earlier in this book, trust is important when working within hybrid work models, with leaders playing an important role in establishing trust at work because they set the tone for trust through openly and honestly sharing information, providing regular feedback, and encouraging open communication (Lewis, 2025). Reliability, integrity, and fairness are key factors for establishing trust and creating a climate of safety where people can express themselves openly and take risks (see Chapter 4).

Sadly, some companies focus more on mistrust and the threat of workers being off task, using technological surveillance tools such as cameras and tracking software. These tools can track login times and productivity, time online, can log keystrokes, monitor screen activity or workers movements using GPS tracking. While these tools help managers ensure that workers are on task, they usually create feelings of mistrust and may hinder honest and open communication overall. A recent study (Nurhidayah & Muliansyah, 2024) concluded that workers are more engaged when they perceive their managers to be trustworthy and reliable suggesting that trust must be a two-way process in hybrid work. An environment of mistrust where workers feel overly monitored might lead to manipulation of surveillance tools such as altering time settings, doing non-work activities on an alternative device, or simulating keyboard and mouse activity. Obviously, none of this is ideal so it seems imperative that if a company and its managers permit hybrid working that it operates within a system of trust and respect. In essence this is where the hybrid system has real strength because workers can work independently some of the time and spend some days in the office getting feedback and guidance on their productivity and performance.

To have the ability to work in a hybrid model implies trust in workers and all of the research participants reinforced this point. The benefits of feeling trusted at work usually flow on to positive work behaviours and improved job performance (Baer et al., 2021). Exemplifying this, Irene emphasises the importance of trust in hybrid working and her increased productivity when she works from home (alone):

> I prefer working from home because I'm more productive there. Yeah, I do feel stress when I'm around people. As much as I love them. I love them so much, but I prefer to be away from a crowd… it's just about trust …trust. If you don't trust your employee, why employ them? (Irene, Firefly).

The issues and complexities of hybrid work suggest that trust needs to be established through clear guidelines about expectations and best practices in order to create clarity and consistency for all workers. Ideally, this could be negotiated between managers and workers when setting up the protocols for hybrid work. And yes, it is a good idea to work out some operational rules and protocols for hybrid workers to assist with clarity, expectations, and ultimately, foster trust and comfort in working flexibly. The companies I researched had gone as far as developing policies for hybrid work and the most significant aspect was the clear guidelines around how many days could be worked from an alternative location (mostly home) and how many days workers needed to be present in the office. Interestingly, although these expectations were clearly articulated in policies, workers still told me that they worked more flexibly than the policy rules stated and varied their number of days in the office and at home depending on work projects, how they were feeling, and what suited them best. All indicated that their managers were fine with this and rarely, if ever, enforced the policy guidelines as long as workers kept them up to date with where they were working and their on-going progress, and they joined online meetings as required. Mostly the hybrid model operated on the principle of trust with some underpinning policy guidelines.

Regular check-ins are useful, and, in both companies where I did my research, they devised 'anchor days' which were nominated days where all staff were expected to attend meetings in the office to update company developments and reinforce expectations. This helped to maintain strong connections with all members of the team and fostered company connectedness. In the Gecko company these meetings were much anticipated, occurred at 9.30 in the morning and the managers organised a tasty breakfast for the all-staff anchor meetings. The meetings that I attended had boxes laden with bagels and a variety of tasty toppings, along with good quality coffee and other drinks. This created goodwill and enthusiasm among the staff and the meeting operated as a real bonding and reconnection session, with workers and managers catching up, chatting, and laughing before getting down to the serious business of the meeting. From this I concluded that hybrid work was well-supported and running smoothly in Gecko, and was powered by trust, reciprocity, and goodwill. Social and food-related treats for attending the office in person were strong incentives to turn-up, reconnect, and this effectively reinforced team and company culture in a warm, fun vibe. This was a happy meeting, enjoyed by all.

Balancing Connection and Disconnection

Regular check—ins can help maintain unity and connection in work teams and many teams are creative when developing virtual social events to foster camaraderie and connection. This is an important aspect of hybrid work because meaningful work relationships are important to workers (Urrila et al., 2025). Examples of activities that foster the relational aspects of work include online games and quizzes, coffee chats, celebrations, casual chats before meetings and these replicate some of the spontaneous interactions that form the social fabric of work life. Social interactions are good for connection as they build relationships, reduce stress, spark ideas and creativity, boost engagement, and offer a more personal communication that helps to foster trust and understanding. Social interaction is an important part of our humanity and often a source of enjoyment at work.

Although some of this social interaction can be achieved via online platforms and video calls, the casual spontaneity of the corridor chat may be lost in hybrid work which can create feelings of isolation and exclusion if others are meeting in person. Online conversations are usually more intentional and therefore more focused on work matters. This is one of the biggest concerns about remote and hybrid work, that casual chats disappear, leaving workers feeling disconnected from some of the more enjoyable social aspects of working life. Furthermore, miscommunication can occur if workers miss out on the informal chats. Traditionally known as 'water cooler' chats, in my academic department, we call these 'corridor conversations' and some of our best ideas and collaborations occur here. When discussing hybrid work Philip identified his loss of connection when working remotely:

> But the time that I spend at work, that cross pollination, of information, of sharing of knowledge of getting to know people and developing relationships that's lost in that hybrid environment, because as you say, I'm on a zoom call, I'm all for zoom calls but there's no niceties. There's no getting to know somebody, it's all business, right (Philip, Sales Manager).

Social chats also offer a good chance to check on work mates' health and wellbeing and share life events - both happy and sad. People are highly relational and social, enjoy stories and warm exchanges and sharing these with colleague can create a shared identity and community through authentic connection and communication. All of this has positive impacts for mental and emotional well-being through making each other feel valued and creating a sense of belonging. For some people, these aspects of work are the most important features—or they at least rank as highly as some work tasks. All of the people I have talked to mention these features of work especially when discussing fun at work or hybrid work set-ups. Very rarely does a person admit that they are disinterested in the social benefits of work and social interaction with colleagues (although I have met a very few who do just want to get their job done without distraction).

Boundaries Matter

One of the challenges faced in hybrid work is the flexible boundaries that separate work and home life (Chan & Kinman, 2024). Clear boundaries are essential because workers can struggle to disconnect from work and may fail to take breaks and leisure time needed to maintain their wellbeing and equilibrium. It is quite common for workers to overwork themselves in hybrid work because their work is always just a few steps away and it is easy to keep working online beyond normal work hours. Therefore, hybrid work requires a thoughtful approach to balance the benefits of flexibility with the ability to connect when needed but just as importantly to consciously disconnect from work at day's end. Jason notes this difficulty in disconnecting from work at the end of the day, so he prefers to work in the office. He also likes the clear guidelines that Gecko have developed governing hybrid work where he must come into work on Tuesday and can choose at least one more day to work in the office. Jason also has the flexibility to work in the office every day or most days if that suits him best even though policy allows him to work only two days in the office—if this is his preference.

> I also don't really like working from home because it's like kind of hard to switch off at the end of the day. And it's yeah, and it's like clear boundaries… cause the days that we have to work from the office are Tuesday and then depending on what squad you're in you choose what day you want to come in (Jason, Gecko).

During the Covid19 pandemic, New Zealand was one of the first countries to go into lockdown on March 25, 2020, following China's

Hubei province and Italy's nationwide lockdown in early March. New Zealand was noted globally for its strict measures and early actions to manage the pandemic. Following this first lockdown, senior staff from my department compiled an edited management book, where researchers were invited to write and submit a chapter about management in the pandemic (Husted & Sinkovics, 2021). I wrote a chapter for this collaborative book called: '*The Lighter Side of Lockdown*' (Plester, 2021) and I included stories that had been told to me about amusing incidents when colleagues had been forced to work remotely using technology. A key message from this chapter was that connecting online with colleagues carries a few risks and video conferencing technology gives colleagues access to your home life and family members, quite often inadvertently. Colleagues recounted stories of forgetting to use a filter and then realising that large piles of washing were visible in meetings. Children featured in these stories and in several cases had wandered into view of the screen doing things that were unusual and often funny. For example, one child had wrapped their feather bed quilt around them before wandering into view. They continued to wind the quilt tighter and tighter until it burst, and the room and screen was a riot of feathers. The colleague who experienced this laughed at the memory but also note the embarrassment that it had occurred in her work meeting.

The point here is that connecting to work via technological devices can sometimes have unexpected factors that give colleagues glimpses of each other's home or family life, in effect, blurring the boundary between work and home. Personally, I am lucky to work in a secluded space and use a distortion background in case I have left anything personal visible. However, my two large dogs like to join me in my home workspace. They are not usually visible in online meetings but have occasionally espied another dog from the window and a cacophony of barking ensues, sometimes just after I have unmuted my microphone to speak. Usually, it is a funny moment that I can get through with a laugh and simple apology and as colleagues have mostly experienced these sorts of interruptions in their own technological communication they are quick to forgive. Most workers do their best to work uninterrupted but depending on circumstances, living spaces, family demands, this can be an aspect of remote work that needs managing and addressing. It comes down to the culture of the organisation or group you work with, your own preferences, your home and family situation, and the resources you have available for hybrid work. Ideally, a company will help set you up with the technological tools and hardware to ensure a (mostly) seamless remote work environment.

'Gerald You're on Mute!'

One quote from a CEO that has stayed with me throughout my research project was when he called online meetings 'the new awkward' and laughingly reminded me of how two people go to speak at the same time then each defers to the other saying 'no - you go - no you'. I am sure this sort of meeting behaviour is familiar to most of you. Raising the virtual hand then when invited to speak, forgetting to unmute and everyone starts gesticulating and shouting 'turn on your mic' 'you're on mute'. Most of us know this scenario and it still happens even when we are seasoned at online communication. The awkwardness of online meetings can result in some people being hesitant to speak and choosing non-participation during these meetings. People can also opt out of fully participating during in-person meetings which somehow seems a little easier to do when positioned behind a screen with the mute option and the ability to turn off your camera.

Even with our advanced technology it is also possible to experience poor internet connection, power failures, software glitches—all incidences that can disrupt communication and make meetings frustrating. I have frequently experienced colleagues saying 'I'll just leave and come back in again'—something that does not usually happen during in-person meetings—unless you've forgotten something important. Added to technological issues is the lack of non-verbal cues, which while still visible on-screen, may be harder to interpret and can be completely masked by simply turning off the camera. Turning off the camera in itself could be considered a non-verbal cue that may be interpreted in many ways—from something to hide—to lack of engagement or doing something else. In technology—supported communication there is more opportunity for mixed messages and misunderstandings that may not be reconciled during the meeting.

Online meetings set the scene for some funny moments as noted in the 'you're on mute struggle'. Added to this is the opportunity for surprise guests such as pets (usually thoroughly enjoyed by colleagues) and the risk of talking while the screen has frozen. Pitfalls such as choosing a busy, over—enthusiastic background can create amusing distractions for those in the meeting or can work as a fun icebreaker in some situations.

Forgetting the mic is still on may create embarrassing faux pas if something untoward is revealed. You may even be caught out multitasking, accidentally revealing a host of other activities you are carrying out while the meeting is on. Most of these situations are happily resolved with a little humour and goodwill which can even enhance communication and collegiality.

Surviving Hybrid Like a Boss

In-person meetings are still my own preference especially when they discuss complex or even personal aspects of working life. For example, while writing this section I was simultaneously responding to a colleague's request to meet for some advice and help with a personal health-related matter that falls within my portfolio of responsibility. My immediate instinct was to meet in-person, but they suggested an online meeting was preferable to them. Immediately I started to recalibrate how we would interact and share sensitive information successfully and although I wasn't as comfortable this way, I am improving my skills and capabilities through constant hybrid work and meeting the needs of others. Happily, it was a successful and productive online meeting.

Participants in the research also pointed out this tension between the desire to meet in-person to enhance the quality of the meeting, versus the convenience of meeting online in hybrid work. They tended to balance it fairly successfully, organising some in-person meetings for days in the office depending on the topic and purpose of the meeting, while holding some meetings online when working from home. Workers that meet with colleagues from different countries, often spanning different time zones, were especially glad of the option of online meetings—even if they had to meet late at night or early morning, although some did complain that it extended their working day significantly.

From the funny, embarrassing and distracting examples above we can infer some useful practices for enhancing our online meetings when working from home or elsewhere. So here are a few pointers developed from working with participants and colleagues.

> Set the agenda and take note of what type of meeting you will be involved with. If everyone understands in advance what to expect, things will progress more effectively. Of course, this is just as important in face-to-face meetings, but I do find I need to think through a meeting more if it

will be an online one as, like the research participants, I struggle with some of the interpersonal cues such as body language being missing or reduced in the online experience.

Choose the right platform for the online meeting because different platforms operate differently and have different expectations embedded. For instance, a meeting organised on Kahoot, Slack or Facetime may imply light-heartedness, fun, games and sociality. Slack has a feature called 'Huddles' for quick discussions or exchanges of ideas or catch-ups for people engaging on the platform. In contrast a more formal, serious and focused online meeting is more commonly conducted on platforms such as Teams, Zoom, Google Meet, Cisco Webex to name a few.

An icebreaker such as a fun question or a check-in at the start of a meeting can make interactions more comfortable and help with resolving small technical glitches such as non-functioning mics and cameras.

In meetings of more than one other person I always mute my mic when I am not speaking which reduces the possibility of background noises and other household distractions. I am lucky enough to have an office space (it is also a spare bedroom) where I can withdraw from family life to participate in meetings. If you don't have a designated space at least warning others in your household that you will be in a meeting might help reduce interruptions and intrusions.

One of the wonderful things about online meetings is that they usually stick to the allocated timeframes as they are electronically scheduled and timing is part of the meeting set-up. It also seems easier to quietly exit on time if you have other commitments through simply turning off the mic and camera and hitting the 'leave' button. Your exit time can be communicated to colleagues at the start of the meeting, noting that you will leave at a specific time. It just feels less confronting and less noticeable leaving a meeting this way in contrast to physically walking out of an in-person meeting.

Online meeting platforms offer a chat function and in big meetings this can be a useful way to gather more input and information that can be saved and reviewed later. For some quieter, more introverted people, this is a comfortable way of sharing their ideas and they have time to formulate thoughts through text. They can avoid the risk of framing their point poorly through feeling shy or embarrassed in speaking up. It does tend to mean that you are following several threads during the same meeting – the spoken points and the textual chat but I enjoy this function and find myself responding in the chat if I can't get space to speak up - or I'm feeling a bit unsure of my idea. I especially find this helpful in larger meetings; the side conversations can be valuable even if they are a bit distracting.

A final key point and advantage of online meetings is that it is very simple to record the session and also inform everyone that recording is occurring. This gives you an excellent, accurate record for minutes and review of the content. The downside is that recording may inhibit some participants in meetings disinclining them from making comments and suggestions, so you may choose not to activate this function, again depending on the purpose of the meeting.

Hybrid work is made possible and enhanced by the right technology. Technology is improving constantly and quickly, and the eruption of Artificial Intelligence (AI) into the work sphere and global markets will add multiple new dimensions that we are still discovering. Will we need to even meet online, or will this function be addressed in other technological ways? Will online platforms evolve further to even more closely replicate in-person communication? Will other, newer tech tools be developed that add to our connections and meetings in alternative ways? Will we need to learn new skills and ways of operating in the technological work environment? Will new issues arise that we haven't considered as yet?

The answer to all or most of these questions is realistically 'yes'. So, I leave this chapter in a place of indecision with multiple questions but also with an openness to what comes next. Writing a chapter on technology runs the risk of being outdated even before completing it, but that is the intrinsic nature of our current tech environment. The hybrid work of tomorrow will be driven by technology that supports and enhances work while adapting and reimagining the very nature of our future collaboration and communication. Bring it on!

References

Baer, M. D., Frank, E. L., Matta, F. K., Luciano, M. M., & Wellman, N. (2021). Undertrusted, overtrusted, or just right? The fairness of (in) congruence between trust wanted and trust received. *Academy of Management Journal, 64*(1), 180–206.

Chan, X. W. C., & Kinman, G. (2024). Work and non-work boundary management including remote and hybrid working. In *Wellbeing at Work in a Turbulent Era* (pp. 56–75). Edward Elgar Publishing.

Husted, K., & Sinkovics, R. R. (Eds.). (2021). Management perspectives on the Covid-19 crisis: Lessons from New Zealand. Edward Elgar Publishing.

Lewis, A. (2025). Good leadership? It starts with trust. *Harvard Business Publishing*. How Leaders Build Trust | Harvard Business Impact. Retrieved July 10, 2025, from https://www.harvardbusiness.org/insight/good-leadership-it-all-starts-with-trust/

Nurhidayah, R., & Muliansyah, D. (2024). Digital leadership and employee engagement in hybrid work environments: The role of trust and communication. *RIGGS: Journal of Artificial Intelligence and Digital Business, 3*(2), 23–33.

Plester, B.A. (2021). The lighter side of lockdown in Kenneth Husted and Rudolf Sinkovics (Eds.) *Management Perspectives on the Covid- 19 Crisis: Lesson from New Zealand.* Edward Elgar.

Urrila, L., Siiriäinen, A., Mäkelä, L., & Kangas, H. (2025). Sense of belonging in hybrid work settings. *Journal of Vocational Behavior, 157*, Article 104096.

Van Zoonen, W., Sivunen, A. E., & Blomqvist, K. (2024). Out of sight–Out of trust? An analysis of the mediating role of communication frequency and quality in the relationship between workplace isolation and trust. *European Management Journal, 42*(4), 515–526.

CHAPTER 8

Hybrid Happily Ever After?

THE QUEST NEVER ENDS

I introduced this book by identifying the quest for workplace happiness, positioning it as the holy grail of workplace exploration. In this aspirational quest my focus was specifically upon how happiness might manifest in and through hybrid work. I am not sure that I have fulfilled such an ambitious quest because the social dynamics of work and workplace relationships were revealed to be highly intricate and diverse and are still developing in new ways. The book had to traverse through some chaos and online calamity but also depicted some happiness, fun, lightness, and laughter in the nooks and crannies of peoples' work experiences. It also recounted unhappiness and discontent about some aspects of work life and some so-called fun that caused embarrassment and discomfort.

I outlined many elements and feelings about fun. Fun was big and small, was safe and risky, was enjoyable and confronting, in other words, fun was complex and contradictory and meant different things to different people. Fun was only one factor in what created workplace happiness. Although linked to fun and humour, happiness was also experienced through workplace autonomy, trust, freedom, and flexibility. It seems that people experience happiness through the ability to work in various formats that offer them these factors and give them choices about where, when, and how to work. While some global companies are enacting back-to-the-office mandates, the workers in this study were vehement that hybrid

© The Author(s), under exclusive license to Springer Nature
Singapore Pte Ltd. 2025
B. Plester, *Hybrid Happiness*,
https://doi.org/10.1007/978-981-95-2092-3_8

work is important to their well-being and determined that they definitely want it to continue. The great advantage of hybridity in workplace models is that it offers workers the best of both worlds, some in-office connection and face-to-face interaction, alongside some days working independently from remote locations, most commonly their own homes.

Hybrid work gives workers variety in their work mode as well as saving them from daily commutes that require time and money. Flexibility, autonomy, and negotiated choices make workers happier and well-being is enhanced through feeling trusted, through having more opportunities for leisure and pleasurable activities, and through the ability to care for family and/or pets. A wide range of positive advantages are experienced in hybrid work.

There are disadvantages and issues also. Hybrid work relies heavily on technology for the remote aspects of work—and even the best tech can be unreliable at times. Online work reduces the cues and clues used in fact-to-face communication which can result in miscommunication and confusion. Emotions are hard to discern in online communication especially if it is text based. Emojis can help with this, but these can be overused or also misinterpreted and the meanings for these seem to shift within pop culture, quite rapidly. Fun and humour have changed in the hybrid environment and some of this has gone online requiring adaptation and creativity to create similar joyful effects to previously enjoyed office banter and in-person social exchanges.

Rewind and Recap

This book explores six interlinked topics beginning with fun in flexible work (Chapter 2) and moving into the notion of fun cultures in Chapter 3. These two chapters presented the ideas that hybrid work stimulates challenges and opportunities for different fun experiences at work. People are still motivated to enjoy fun, but workers acknowledge that it is continuously changing and is becoming much more blended as it moves between in-person and online formats. Sensitivity and balance are needed to enjoy fun across online and in-person formats with gamification offering one way of sharing work-focused fun that can be playful, competitive, and hopefully—enjoyable. Companies with fun cultures have experienced challenges in maintaining this specific type of culture in hybrid work, noting that fun is sometimes less spontaneous and physically interactive and that office events have changed through varying attendance when people work in hybrid mode. Key fun activities such as table tennis and Friday after-work drinks have been adapted or scrapped and new types of fun activities such as quizzes, photo comps, and online chats or drink sessions are more prevalent. People and Culture leaders have taken some responsibility for instigating new forms of fun in hybrid work in order to preserve friendly social interaction and team bonding.

Chapter 4 introduced the idea of psychological safety and emphasised the importance of this concept to positive experiences of fun and social interaction at work. Themes regarding risk, authenticity, and leadership were explored as essential elements of the ability to enjoy fun at work. The idea that not all fun activities are enjoyable to all workers was one of the nuanced ideas in this chapter as well as the recognition that psychological safety is important in workplace fun. As hybrid work has increased, the ambiguity of fun has also escalated as it traverses both online and in-person modes, potentially causing new issues and challenges. A psychologically safe workplace climate fosters authenticity, creativity, and self-expression. When workers feel safe in their work culture and climate then spontaneous fun interactions can occur and this improves overall happiness for many workers—both online and in the office—or both.

Emotion was the overarching topic for Chapter 5 and happiness is one of the six key emotions agreed upon by researchers. Workers agreed that having the freedom to work flexibly in hybrid set-ups enhances their wellbeing and happiness by reducing commute time, offering autonomy, and through offering the ability to balance work, home-life, and family responsibilities. Hybrid work implies trust in the individual worker, and this may increase their commitments and effort for the company or organisation. Conversely, back-to-the-office mandates imply a lack of trust in workers that may foster resentment and resistance through the loss of freedom and flexibility. Hybrid work generates mixed emotions ranging from frustration and anxiety to feelings of wellbeing and happiness and these emotional impacts have multiple implications for workers, managers, and organisations.

Chapter 6 explicitly addressed workplace happiness concluding that a culture of trust and respect are important for well-functioning hybrid teams. Being trusted to work autonomously and having the freedom of flexible work engenders greater happiness and higher levels of worker engagement. Developing a hybrid work model requires logistics but more importantly can be a cultural shift empowering workers to balance their personal and professional well-being. Hybrid work models offer a balanced approach that can be optimal if managed well with frequent check-ins, support for mental health, and clear boundaries that allow workers to log-off and disconnect from work at an appropriate time. Team engagement needs continuous fostering, and a plethora of virtual team activities can be accessed online to strengthen relationships through adding some fun and games to the workday. Reward, recognition, and acknowledgement can be maintained to boost morale and uphold positive team dynamics.

Chapter 7 presented the all-important topic of technology which is needed to manage hybrid work. Although we have sophisticated technology available to many workplaces and workers now, this is rapidly changing, and technological progress will engender a whole raft of changes, developments, and upskilling in the near future. We are constantly creating new work problems for technology to solve, but at the same time, technology is generating new ways of working that must be embraced in order to keep up and stay relevant in modern work. Hybrid and technological intelligence will be vital future skills.

Hybrid Intelligence: Tomorrow's Workplace Weapon

Hybrid work as we currently understand it will need to evolve to meet the challenge of in-person and virtual interactions that will also incorporate human-AI interaction in virtual realms (Richter & Richter, 2024). The rapid rise of AI is reshaping hybrid work already as it blends automation with flexibility. This could mean more emphasis on tasks that require emotional intelligence and creativity as AI handles more of the mundane tasks. It seems likely that jobs will increasingly use AI insights and information to interpret development and make informed decisions. There will be challenges as companies will need to embed ethical practices into AI use, such as ensuring inclusive practices to so that AI benefits everyone.

Workers will need AI literacy and fluency and will need to know how to use it effectively with an understanding of what it can, and cannot, do. We are entering a new era of collaboration between humans and systems, and we need to find ways for AI to amplify human strengths. Critical thinking will be even more necessary, and workers will need to embrace continuous learning and experimentation while maintaining human connection. AI fluency is fast becoming a fundamental workplace attribute in recruitment decisions, but the human skills of communication and relationship building are even more relevant in an AI powered future (Marr, 2025). In my own academic career, AI has already completely changed the landscape for assessing student work, planning and delivery of learning, and considerations of diversity and inclusion. Educational priorities will continue to evolve quickly as tertiary institutions work out how to harness AI, use it with students, and teach students strong and ethical practices for AI use that they can take into their graduate careers and tech-powered futures. Students have been quick to adopt AI so along with their knowledge and understanding of different formats and platforms, we need to ensure that critical thinking, complex problem-solving, integrity, and ethics are fully preserved and enhanced. The AI we have now is merely the beginning and keeping up with future development will require collaboration, impactful teaching, and practical application of this and forthcoming technological advances (Hansen, 2025). It seems that meeting these (not-too-distant) future challenges will require hybrid intelligence that involves complexity, learning, reasoning and adaptive action—in other words an intelligence that combines the complementary intelligence of both humans and machines (Dellerman et al., 2019).

Humour and fun cannot, and will not, disappear in the AI-fuelled workplace. Chatbots can already do banter and be light-hearted. AI can bring up trivia and quirky questions to kick off meetings or team sessions. Gamification is rife, exciting, and easily available to those with an interest in this aspect of work life. AI can be asked for silly ideas—I know—I asked it while I was writing this book. It offered me a mood-boosting nudge to overcome a mid-afternoon slump, even giving itself the name BreezyBot:

BreezyBot:
Fun fact: sloths can hold their breath longer than dolphins. That has absolutely nothing to do with your inbox - but hopefully it made you smile. Now back to conquering the digital jungle! 🌴💻(Microsoft co-pilot)

So perhaps AI is one key to our future fun and happiness along with our continuing human interactions and social dynamics—in essence a human-tech hybridity. I fervently hope it can help create and maintain future workplace hybrid happiness.

References

Dellermann, D., Ebel, P., Söllner, M., & Leimeister, J. M. (2019). Hybrid intelligence. *Business & Information Systems Engineering, 61*(5), 637–643.

Hansen, M. (2025). The New Learning Curve: Adapting Education for An AI-Driven World. *Forbes.com*. Accessed 10/07/2025.

Marr, B. (2025). The Essential Skills That Will Define Success In The AI Era (And They're Not What You Think). Retrieved July 10, 2025, from www.forbes.com

Richter, A., & Richter, S. (2024). Hybrid work–a reconceptualisation and research agenda. *i-com, 23*(1), 71–78.

GPSR Compliance
The European Union's (EU) General Product Safety Regulation (GPSR) is a set of rules that requires consumer products to be safe and our obligations to ensure this.

If you have any concerns about our products, you can contact us on

ProductSafety@springernature.com

In case Publisher is established outside the EU, the EU authorized representative is:

Springer Nature Customer Service Center GmbH
Europaplatz 3
69115 Heidelberg, Germany

www.ingramcontent.com/pod-product-compliance
Lightning Source LLC
LaVergne TN
LVHW020413070526
838199LV00054B/3603